An American Epidemic

An American Epidemic

Mortgage Fraud—A Serious Business

By Michael S. Richardson,
www.preventmortgagefraud.com

iUniverse, Inc.
New York Lincoln Shanghai

An American Epidemic
Mortgage Fraud—A Serious Business

Copyright © 2005 by Michael S. Richardson

iUniverse books may be ordered through booksellers or by contacting:

iUniverse
2021 Pine Lake Road, Suite 100
Lincoln, NE 68512
www.iuniverse.com
1-800-Authors (1-800-288-4677)

Legal Disclaimer:
The contents of this book are NOT a substitute for the advice of an attorney.
You should seek independent and competent legal counsel before acting
(or refraining from acting) upon any of the information contained in this book.

ISBN-13: 978-0-595-37237-9 (pbk)
ISBN-13: 978-0-595-81635-4 (ebk)
ISBN-10: 0-595-37237-6 (pbk)
ISBN-10: 0-595-81635-5 (ebk)

Printed in the United States of America

Dedication and Acknowledgments

This book would not be possible without the loving support of so many people to whom I am forever indebted. As a man who is usually not too full of words, I find myself overwhelmed at the thought of offering them all my thanks in dedicating this book to them.

To my wife, Kim, who, after 25 years of love and support and married life together, as well as being business partners for the same 25 years—she is my strength and purpose in life. With no exception nothing is more important. I love you, Kim, now and forever.

To my children, Ryan, Sarah, and her husband, Dalyn, as well as my grandson, Hunter, who are my inspiration when life looks dreary and I am not sure what to do next. They are the reason I find my way to the decency in people and life again, but as they have gotten older I know they are there to help me with the burden of steering our family past the rough waters when I need them the most.

To my mother and father; my dad gave me the model of life that I live to this day to be trusting in people. And to my mom, my friend, #1 supporter, and both of them so much more—they have both always supported my decisions in life with positive care and love.

To my father-in-law, Donald L. Rieder, who left this life much too soon—and far too young. In his time with us, Don not only lived life to its fullest, he was my business mentor for 23 years. He was the most creative, optimistic businessman I have ever known. I learned my business morals and principles from him. He taught me that no matter how dreadful a business situation looks to always find the good and the positive in order to solve the problem; work on the situation relentlessly and you will land on your feet one step ahead of where you started. In his 15 months of battling brain cancer (no matter how painful), he continued to live life to its fullest, finding a reason to get out of bed every day and accomplish something positive and optimistic, no matter how small. I only wish he was here to read my book.

To my other family members and friends, I was going to start listing them all, but realized there are just too many to do them all justice—so please accept the fact that you are all mentioned in my thoughts of thanks and I will continue on a daily basis to look for the best in you and convey my thanks when we spend time together.

Contents

A Brief Excerpt from *American Epidemic*

Would you ever say the "F" word in public? Do you even dare to bring the "F" word up in polite conversation? After all, if you even mention the "F" word it makes any honest, hard working real estate professional quiver. The "F" word is a dirty word in the mortgage industry, and for good reason.

So, have you guessed it yet? What, exactly, IS the "F" word?

"Fraud."

More specifically: "Mortgage Fraud."

Don't get me wrong: fraud isn't a factor in every mortgage loan, or even in every branch, but the outcome of even one fraudulent loan can affect the entire industry, in general, and individual practitioners, in particular.

The ripple effect of fraud is as deep as it is far-reaching. The mortgage lenders and borrowers stand to lose much more than the cost of the damages when fraud appears. At risk is their very reputation in the industry. And as all of us know, in THIS industry our word is our bond; our reputation is our bread and butter.

Who can afford to lose that precious commodity?

Where does mortgage fraud begin and how do we prevent—or at least begin to stop—mortgage fraud? They say timing is everything, and in this case there's never been a better time to commit—or fall prey to—mortgage fraud. The unprecedented real estate boom over the last few years, which led to the doubly dangerous refinancing craze that subsequently swept the nation, has contributed substantially to the rise in mortgage fraud.

This one-two double-whammy has sucker-punched its share of consumers, resulting in widespread appraisal fraud whereby property values are greatly—and unjustifiably—inflated to prey on the unsophisticated buyer, who is then left holding the note on a property worth but a fraction of the value at which it had been improperly appraised.

Of course, that's just what happens on the consumer end. How can we, as practitioners working within the industry, control our end of the mortgage fraud equation? Unfortunately, the problem is as internal as it is systemic.

According to Lew Schielman, a popular columnist for <u>www.landlord.com</u>, "For the most part…the perpetrator isn't a professional thief—or even the borrower—it's one or more of the dozen or so specialists—the loan officer, appraiser, real estate agent, title agent—who touches the mortgage as it winds its way through the approval process. Most cases—80 percent by one estimate—involve insiders…"

Is it any wonder? After all, loan originators and their team members have detailed access to the borrower's information in the transaction. From social security numbers to bank account information, it's all above board and on the table. Many of us treat such information as sacrosanct, keeping it under lock and key and using it for one purpose and one purpose only. To those who would perpetrate fraud, however, such information becomes the key they use to unlock the door to fraud.

Every part of the mortgage lending process presents another window of opportunity to unscrupulous loan originators, who by the very nature of their job description come in contact with builders, real estate agents, borrowers, processors, underwriters, appraisers, lender account reps, and title closers.

Each one of these positions or areas needed to get a mortgage leaves an opportunity for fraud!

About This Book:
An American Epidemic

"Over the past decade, real estate fraud has grown to become one of the most significant threats to profitability in the residential mortgage banking industry…"

~ **Steve Schroeder, founder and CEO of C & S Marketing**

The American Epidemic. Consider that title for a moment. Epidemic may sound like a strong word to you, but after considering the latest figures on real estate fraud it is my sincere belief that you will feel the word isn't quite strong enough!

According to the FBI's May 2005 Financial Crimes Report to the Public, the number of mortgage fraud reports filed has escalated nearly 150% since 2003. The report also showed that 80% of the cases involve either overstated property appraisals or non-existent properties.

Fraud. Clearly, the statistics point to nothing short of an epidemic. And yet, really, what do we know about fraud? In point of fact, it's not what we know about fraud that's dangerous; it's what we *don't* know. What's worse is the staggering amount of opportunity with which the American real estate industry provides those who commit fraud.

According to the Mortgage Bankers of America, or MBA, their 2005 Mortgage Originations forecast estimates some $2,738,000,000,000 (that extra trio of zeroes isn't a typo; that's over 2 *trillion* dollars!) in new loans.

This staggering number includes the approximately 20 million in home mortgages required to cover refinanced loans, new home sales and existing home sales. Those are big numbers, and now even the MBA is including the likelihood of fraud in their statistics, estimating that 10% to15% of mortgage loans have some kind of fraud involved. This means that between 2 to 3 million home loans originated this year could be fraudulent; that equates to over 7,500 new fraudulent loans *every business day.*

Now that *is* an epidemic…

Who benefits from such fraud? By my own calculations based on such industry standards, loan officers and others involved in the mortgage transaction will generate roughly over $8 billion in fraudulent loan fees while real estate companies and agents themselves will rake in over $13 billion in commissions from these fraudulent transactions. Now, while I am not insinuating the real estate agents are all involved in fraudulent transactions, I do think that it's important to show readers that the agents have a lot to lose if these loans are not closed.

The statistics on fraud may be sobering, but what's worse is the sparse amount of stop-gap measures currently in place to prevent this all too common felony. Many of us come to the industry by way of other careers. With the real estate market growing exponentially, and the resulting refinance craze over the last few years, it is not uncommon for us to be working alongside relative newcomers from careers as diverse as education, law enforcement, medicine, the automotive industry and even the retail, hospitality, and entertainment fields.

Clearly, the amount of money to be made in real estate—both residential and commercial—lends itself to abuse. New employees mean new training, and lack of new training leads to old mistakes. The growth of fraud is insidious; it creeps up on us, taking us by surprise until, before we know it, someone we work with, someone we work for, or even those who work for us, is committing fraud.

It's so easy, so slick, and until now so largely un-enforced. A number fudged there, a figure left out here, a bogus appraisal, a friend of a friend who plays it fast and loose with a client's verification of rent, a fabricated credit report, and soon enough a mortgage loan is fraudulent.

Once a white-collar criminal gets away with it, the process quickly becomes addictive. Success breeds more success, and before long such crafters of fraudulent mortgage loans clearly begin feeling that not only are they above the law but, in fact, they aren't doing anything wrong in the first place.

But those of us who take our profession seriously, who are in this business to help sincere, hardworking, law-abiding citizens obtain housing in a fair market for a mortgage that works for them can think of little worse than those who prey on the innocent, the righteous, the unsophisticated and the trusting.

Fraud can happen to anyone: loan officers, processors, underwriters, buyers, sellers, investors, owners and management of mortgage companies. It can happen anywhere: big cities, small towns, storied and well-recognized firms and smaller mom and pop businesses who just want to do the right thing.

So, who still thinks "epidemic" is too harsh a word?!?

Don't let the statistics get you down, though: according to the Mortgage Bankers Association of America, "…the U.S. Attorney and others have suggested that as much as 70–80 percent of mortgage fraud *can* be avoided through aggressive fraud awareness and detection efforts."

That's where I come in. My personal experiences with mortgage fraud, which you'll learn about shortly, have given me a doctoral degree from the school of hard knocks. Much like you, I "never thought it could happen to me."

But it did.

It can.

And if the statistics prove out, it probably will…

But it doesn't have to. Not to you, anyway. And not to those you do business with. In fact, in this book I am going to give you all the tools you'll need to protect yourself from becoming a victim of this increasingly common crime.

On the following pages you will learn:

- **How to Start Closing the Door on Fraud**
- **Realizing the Scope of the Problem**
- **The 2 Types of Mortgage Fraud**
- **Common Loan Fraud**
- **Understanding the Whole Transaction**
- **Hot Fraud Schemes**
- **Stopping the Paper Trail**
- **Where Fraud Originates**
- **What to Look Out For**
- **Buzz Words**
- **How the Bad Guys Operate**
- **What They Say to Get the Fraud Done**
- **How to Recognize Loan Fraud**

This is no textbook. The language I'll use is simple and straightforward. Not only have I been there and done that, but I've also paid for the crimes of those who've done so without my knowledge. You will be able to profit from my mistakes, my naiveté, and my inexperience in dealing with criminals who know exactly how to work the system, and make others like you and I pay for their crimes.

I'll take you through a real-life scam, from beginning to end, sharing with you along the way my own experiences and what I learned to do, what I should have done, and what I wish I'd done earlier. By the time our journey together is over you will be fully-equipped to spot, assess, recognize, and best of all *prevent* mortgage fraud from happening to you.

First, however, I'd like to share with you my own personal story and how I came to be such an expert on real estate fraud. I promise it won't be long, and in fact I'm almost positive that as I tell my story you'll soon be nodding your head in recognition.

My Story, or:
Why I'm Qualified to Write This Book

"Because of what they do, mortgage loan processors have access to a lot of personal information—names, birth dates, Social Security numbers and more. But in the wrong hands, it can be used in nefarious ways..."

~ Patrick Crowley, www.MortgageDaily.com

They say when one door closes a window typically opens, giving you a chance to turn failure into opportunity or, as they also say, make lemons into lemonade. But they don't say anything about the size of the window that needs to open when not just one but ALL the doors shut, or when all the doors shut, the walls fall down, and the roof caves in on the very same day!

What are you supposed to do *then*?!? What window is big enough to climb through when you're dragging the baggage of a ruined reputation, dozens of confused employees, and clients wondering about the status of their perhaps fraudulent mortgages?

I say all this not to sound bitter but to describe for you the feeling I had on March 21, 2005, the day the doors seemed to shut on my company and myself. The day I learned that I had been not only the victim of mortgage fraud but according to my accusers, a possible key player in committing said fraud.

The day, in effect, all the doors of my life slammed shut at once...

It was a mild spring day by Colorado standards, and I arrived at work with the typical stresses and hopes of a small business owner riding on my shoulders. I walked through the halls of my office suite, proud of what I'd been able to accomplish in nearly 20 years of working in the real estate mortgage business.

After working in the industry for sixteen years I had formed my third mortgage company, Primero Home Loan, after successfully owning two other companies dating back to 1989 and had profitably sold my first two companies.

My new company, Primero, was a retail loan correspondent that originated and processed loans. Basically, Primero assisted applicants with completing loan applications and then compiled the additional documentation and information needed by an investor to underwrite a loan (i.e.: credit reports, appraisals, W-2 forms, pay stubs, etc.).

After these documents were obtained, the loan officer and loan processor packaged the information according to an investor's specific guidelines and sent the information to underwriting for approval.

It was the perfect opportunity for me to use my industry expertise to facilitate the approval of hundreds, if not thousands, of mortgages per year, and I did so by hiring, training, and supervising a network of qualified employees who believed in our company and what we did.

It wasn't easy owning my own business. Every day, or so it seemed, there were a dozen brush fires to put out and the minute one was extinguished another popped up right beside it. Still, I'd managed to build a solid company in a competitive industry, and up to that point my reputation was as unsullied as our many customers were satisfied.

For nearly two decades I steered my businesses through financial ups and downs, watching the bond market and feds raise and lower interest rates like my own personal real estate roller coaster. (Sound familiar?)

I managed to weather more than my share of storms and, in the spring of 2005, was riding high on a record number of both new and existing home loans, as well as my fair share of refinances. Much like the healthy spring flowers were popping up everywhere, the real estate sales were in full bloom that bright and temperate morning in March as I walked to my office, but little did I know it was my world, and not the housing market, that was about to burst.

A letter was waiting for me on my desk, and instantly I recognized the familiar HUD stationary. The Department of Housing and Urban Development, better known as HUD, was a huge part of my business, accounting for up to 75 % of Primero's mortgage originations. We got mail from them all the time; an update here, a new policy initiative there, but a small part of me had been expecting a negative letter from HUD based on our current default ratio posted on the HUD neighborhood watch web site. Still, with all the work we had been doing since last year to mitigate the loans, I did not have reason to feel alarm as I went about my morning routine that day; after all, I had not done anything unethical or illegal.

In fact, I barely gave it another thought…

After booting up my computer, listening to some messages, returning some calls, and pouring myself a cup of coffee, I finally settled in to read the morning mail. It was then that my attention turned, at long last, to the letter from HUD. Hoping and expecting another update or correction, to be filed away for future reference, I learned instead that HUD was, in fact, notifying Primero of its intention to "terminate its Origination Approval Agreement because of its default and claim rates on HUD/FHA insured mortgages…"

As one might imagine, I was devastated. Since opening Primero Home Loans two years earlier—and after owning two other mortgage companies that were approved to issue HUD/FHA loans and did not have any problems with early default or claim rates—the letter seemed particularly unjustified. Why, I had even received a Best Practices award from HUD in 1997. I was confused, to say the least. Didn't they know my company was just the conduit for these loans?

More questions followed: "How could HUD think the fraud had originated with *us*?!?" I wondered.

In fact, it was the wholesale lending investor underwriting department, not Primero, which determined the final approval and gave us the "clear to close" on whether a borrower qualified for a loan under the lender's guidelines. As is the case with most businesses of its kind, Primero did not fund loans or make the final determinations regarding a borrower's loan eligibility, nor did we actually fund the loans. We worked with approximately nineteen different wholesale investors. Individual loan officers working for Primero determined which investors to pre-approve borrowers with—and close the loans with—on specific transactions.

The news set off a ripple effect through my already reeling brain. Such a decree from HUD would be a crucial blow to our monthly volumes and revenues, but what pained me the most was the shame I felt at receiving such a letter, particularly when I'd done nothing to deserve it and did not knowingly participate in the fraud committed. HUD was terminating us due to our default comparison ratio, which was a direct result of the fraudulent loans originated and closed the year before.

After all, this was not some phony shell corporation or business front; Primero was my pride and joy, a company in which I'd invested endless amounts of money, blood, sweat, and tears over the past two years; starting and operating what I had decided to be my final company until my retirement days.

Now, with a single letter, HUD was basically accusing ME of fraud. My stomach lurched and suddenly I was in no mood for the cup coffee cooling on top of my desk. Still, despite the jittery nerves and gloomy financial forecast for Primero, there was an ironic sense of smugness that filled me that morning.

I knew I hadn't committed fraud. In some small way, this measure of intestinal fortitude gave me the resolve I needed to fight HUD's decision tooth and nail. I would need every ounce of pride, resolve, and emotional follow through I had in the coming months, but of course I didn't know that then.

I thought for sure there had been a mistake; a reporting error of defaulted loans in one or more departments or a computer glitch that transposed my company name and address onto some other company's wrongdoings. HUD was a branch of the US government, after all. Wasn't it more likely that one of the country's biggest and widespread government institutions made a mistake about terminating my company?

A hundred different scenarios went through my mind as I put in a call to my lawyer, then huddled my closest staff, several of which are close family members, including my partner in business and life, my wife, to discuss the implications of the now infamous HUD letter. But the more my staff and I investigated HUD's allegations, the more we realized that something, indeed, was afoot.

And, unfortunately for all of us, it *wasn't* back at HUD…

Things happened quickly after that. I felt like a prison warden who wakes up one morning only to discover that all his inmates have escaped. I'd done nothing wrong but the guilt by association was shameful, depressing, and alarming. I felt betrayed, violated, and taken advantage of.

It had started back in late September 2004, with the quality control of Primero closed loan files. HUD requires mortgage companies to have an audit done on 10% of all mortgage loans closed. Our current quality control company had started sending audit reports with some unusual notations from one of my senior—and highest volume—loan officers. I did not suspect what I eventually found, but the more quality control reports we received and the deeper we dug, the more we realized we were up to our knees in it.

In fact, it soon came to my attention that the misrepresentations and sus- pected fraudulent activities of several (now former) employees of Primero, in conjunction with several underwriters at a couple of national wholesale investors and a customer service representative working for a nationwide credit reporting agency and possibly an appraiser as well, were significant factors contributing to Primero's default and claim rates with HUD, which was the main reason for the termination letter. The news was at once both reassuring and disturbing. We'd found the source of the scam but now we needed to know how far it had spread and how it worked, if that was at all possible.

I felt like a detective solving a crime; to uncover the massive conspiracy that had led to HUD's decision to terminate its Origination Approval Agreement I couldn't just go back a few weeks and months; I had to go back to the very begin- ning. Soon after Primero began its operations, we had contracted for the services of a third party quality control company, Quality QC, to review and audit our loan files after closing.

Every mortgage company is required to perform post-closing quality control and it can be done by a third party or you can have an internal quality control program. We wanted a third party arrangement, so Quality QC became our "go to" guy for all of our quality control.

During the early fall of 2004 I reviewed an audit report from Quality QC and discovered that some of the credit reports in Primero's loan files were different from what Quality QC had downloaded from Reliable Credit Info's secure website. After reviewing several more loan files over the next few weeks, I was shocked to learn of more fraudulent credit reports and discovered that many of these altered credit reports were contained within the loan files of a single senior loan originator at Primero, a woman named Amy Mead, who had worked for Primero for several years.

Our policy at Primero was that after we received a quality control report, I would sit down with the loan officer and review all issues discovered in the report and document the discussion and resolutions to correct issues for future mortgage originations; basically learn from our mistakes.

On the first few quality control reports we reviewed together, Amy gave me what seemed to be reasonable explanations for why there was such a drastic difference in the two credit reports, such as "we had the bad credit removed because it was a mistake," a particular credit trade line "did not belong to that borrower," etc. Based on her reasonable explanations, I did not think too much more about the issue, but I did inform her that she needed to get some back-up documentation and insert the information in the files, just in case we were ever to be audited by HUD.

The following week we received more quality control reports with very similar issues, so this time I spent a couple of days trying to figure out what was going on. Upon further examination I discovered a file that had just closed that day, October 7, and felt I had enough information to suggest "something bad" was happening with Amy's loan files and that her excuses from earlier where most likely untrue, to say the least.

I sent an email to Ms. Mead instructing her not to obtain any more credit reports from the agency in question and froze her ability to pull credit reports and other online tools needed to originate loans. It sounds like a no-brainer but, in point of fact, it was merely a stopgap measure designed to halt any more immediate brush fires while I probed deeper to find the greater issues at large.

As I suspected, the credit reports were only part of the problem.

Later that evening, I spoke with Ms. Mead over the telephone and informed her that she was being terminated from Primero due to "quality control issues" and suspected misrepresentations and fraud. I also advised her that I was terminating all other individuals who were assisting her in processing and originating loans. This massive house cleaning included several key employees who I later realized had been personally groomed by Ms. Mead to do their appointed jobs, and to do them quite well.

In taking these drastic steps it turned out I was a day late and a dollar short. Now the events of last October were coming back to haunt me. It didn't matter that after October 7, 2004 none of these individuals originated or processed loans for Primero. It didn't matter that I had changed the locks on the doors and computer codes to ensure that none of these individuals could gain access to Primero's office or any of its loan files.

The "mortgage marauders," as I would later come to call them, merely picked up stakes and moved their whole operation elsewhere. Several weeks later, upon learning that Ms. Mead had obtained employment at Mortgage 4 US Company as a loan originator, I called Mortgage 4 US to advise them of what Ms. Mead had done while working for us.

I later learned that Ms. Mead committed fraud while at Mortgage 4 US, even though I had warned them, and was subsequently terminated for her actions there. Within approximately one week of being terminated from Mortgage 4 US, I learned that Ms. Mead had changed her name and obtained employment at yet another company, R 2 Mortgage.

By now I was on to her game: I ended up knowing someone at the wholesale investor and promptly notified them that if they were underwriting a lot of the loans for this new company, to advise them of what Ms. Mead had done while at my company. I was not surprised to learn that Ms. Mead had also committed fraud while at R 2 Mortgage and was subsequently terminated, even though they had been warned.

After analyzing the Mortgage Specific Summary Report attached to HUD's March 21, 2005 Notice of Termination, my staff and I eventually calculated that the majority of the loans HUD had identified as being in default were originated by Ms. Mead and her co-conspirators. It was a crushing blow to my own, as well as the company's, formerly high self-confidence.

It proved to us that if we could get hit, no company was safe. After all, I thought we had a sufficient pre-funding quality control plan in place. We verified social security numbers, we looked up employers on various Internet sources; basically, we covered our bases—and then some. When it came to the individual loans I considered our back up plan to be our wholesale investor, who was underwriting the final loan files to obtain the clear to close. It was like a safety net for us; we felt what we did not catch, they *would*.

Primero was a considerable company in the spring of 2005, based on a mortgage broker status, but I had worked very hard to make sure that it still had a small company feel. We all knew each other, or so we thought, and to be betrayed in such a fashion—and to such a wide-ranging extent—was truly a crushing blow to one and all. Ms. Mead had gone on to wreak considerable havoc at other mortgage loan companies after being terminated from ours. The fact that ours was not the only company she "hit" was of little consolation.

Despite the depressing nature of these almost daily revelations, I was slowly building a case for HUD not to terminate us, and wasted no time in telling them so. (To date this matter is currently being investigated by HUD's Office of Inspector General.) In fact, Primero is fully cooperating with the Special Agent in charge of conducting the investigation. Also, Primero is fully cooperating with the Quality Assurance Division regarding its recent audit of Primero's loan files.

Still, I can't help but think of how much time, energy, and money has been spent defending us against charges that resulted through no fault of our own. (I'll never watch Court TV the same way again!) The many hours spent tracking down Ms. Mead's trail of fraud, attorney costs, re-auditing of loan file costs, consulting fees, the expense of photocopying her paper trail and changing the locks, the hours, days, weeks, and months of momentum lost by giving my energy entirely over to this investigation have been truly demoralizing.

Sadly, this was just the beginning of the story: After learning of the misrepresentations and suspected fraudulent activities of Ms. Mead and her "gang," I began examining *all* of her loan files. Because the falsified credit reports in Ms. Mead's files appeared to be authentic, I suspected that Ms. Mead's contact person at the credit report company she was using at the time, Hope Walker, was also under suspicion of committing fraud by altering credit reports. In fact, now I clearly remembered that Ms. Walker would call our office on a very regular basis just to talk to Ms. Mead.

We now believe that Ms. Mead had a childhood connection with Ms. Walker and that Ms. Walker would delete trade lines from borrowers' credit reports or, as we call it now, "scrub the report clean" and provide falsified credit reports to Ms. Mead. A typical credit report (one where no changes are made) costs $21.00. However, the credit reports that appear to have been altered cost more than the standard amount.

We understand that each time a change is made to a credit report additional charges are automatically assessed. Accordingly, each time Ms. Walker, or someone at her credit reporting company, deleted a trade line or made other changes to credit reports additional charges were billed to Primero. Importantly, there was no documentation in the loan files to support those changes, such as a letter of explanation provided from the borrower, and yet we were being charged more than the standard amount, insinuating that someone made changes to those reports; thus the higher charge for the credit reports.

After I discovered that the credit reports in Ms. Mead's files appeared to have been altered or scrubbed clean by an individual working for Reliable Credit Info,

I spoke with a representative from the company concerning my suspicions and sent a request asking them to investigate the credit reports in question.

The first and only response they gave me was that it must be "cut and paste" issues. I disagreed and tried to explain, but they were not having any of it. They then requested I send some more examples over for them to review, which I did. Despite my further repeated requests, however, Reliable Credit Info never responded again.

Because Reliable Credit Info was the only credit reporting agency that my company was using, all of the loan files originated by Ms. Mead that HUD has identified as in default contained credit reports from Reliable Credit Info. Because these credit reports appeared authentic, there was no reason for Primero to suspect that they had been falsified.

As of today I am not sure of the exact or final amount of fraudulent loans they created, due to the fact that since I received the letter from HUD I cannot access the information needed using the Neighborhood Watch web page where the information is compiled. Further complicating issues is the fact that the investors or payments servicing company has not asked or provided the information for me to continue to help with the loan files.

It seemed incredible to me that the problem could be so systemic. It was the proverbial tar pit: every time I so much as moved, another part of me—and my company—got dirty. At the end of some days I had to ask myself: Was there anyone who *wasn't* involved in the conspiracy?

So far the implication seemed clear: almost every piece of processing and approving a loan in the mortgage transaction had been affected. My investigation revealed that not only had the loan officer (Ms. Mead) and her team of assistants been at the root of the problem, but the wholesale investor mortgage company, the real estate agent, possibly one of the appraisers, but now even the credit reporting agency were all involved!

How far did the conspiracy reach?

The questions did little to solve the problem, though. For Primero to regain its accreditation and trust through HUD, not to mention its good name, it would take answers, not questions; action, not frustration.

And so we acted: after discovering that these credit reports had in fact been altered, we naturally stopped obtaining *any* credit reports from Reliable Credit Info. Also, upon close examination of Ms. Mead's loan files, we discovered that certain underwriters working for the wholesale mortgage investor company were waiving standard closing conditions (or not asking for standard closing conditions) and approving loans giving them the "clear to close" without obtaining the proper required documentation.

Had these underwriters at the wholesale mortgage investor diligently performed their duties by ensuring that each borrower had satisfied the wholesale mortgage investor and FHA's lending criteria, then a majority number of these loans might never have been closed and funded.

We later learned that one of the wholesale mortgage investors was the underwriter on 85% of the loans that were originated by Ms. Mead—and identified on HUD's Mortgage Specific Summary Report.

Who underwrote the other 15%? The second wholesale mortgage investor.

After I suspected that certain underwriters at this wholesale mortgage investor were involved in fraudulently approving loans to close, Primero promptly stopped submitting loans for underwriting. After October 7, 2004, we worked with the wholesale mortgage investor for several months in an attempt to assist us in figuring out what caused the defaults.

At the time I had a strong feeling that I needed to lend a helping hand and wanted to get the loans off of the HUD default list. I had assumed that these borrowers and homeowners would want to keep their homes and needed help in understanding what had happened as well as what was *still* happening.

The spirit of cooperation at this wholesale mortgage investor was more genuine and less strained than at some of the other wholesale mortgage companies I'd encountered when a mortgage was in default. It wasn't until I started to discover some very unusual underwriting approvals that Primero completely stopped working with them.

Today I understand this wholesale mortgage investor has in fact terminated all of the underwriters and the sales representative; the branch manager assigned to Primero's account was also forced to resign based on those involved in approving these loans to close. As befits this ingrained pattern of widespread conspiracy, however, some of the underwriters who were terminated by this wholesale mortgage investor are now working for *other* lenders. I have contacted some of these lenders to advise them of the situation. We have also ceased working with any lenders who are currently employing these individuals.

After uncovering this important information it seems clear now that because the underwriters at the wholesale mortgage investor had a duty to ensure that the documentation contained in the loan files met the guidelines of their company and FHA guidelines prior to funding and because certain underwriters failed to fulfill these duties, a great many of the HUD/FHA loans originated by Primero went into default. It was later discovered that this particular wholesale investor underwrote 75% or more of the loans identified by HUD as in default.

Sadly, they were not alone: at the wholesale mortgage company an unnamed investor funded and served as the underwriter on five of the loans identified as in default on the Mortgage Specific Summary Report. An employee named Sally Joiner served as the underwriter on each of these loans and Ms. Mead originated 80% of these loans.

I firmly believe that Ms. Joiner was wrongfully clearing loans to close by not obtaining new credit reports, as it was known to Primero that all files submitted at the wholesale mortgage investor #2 would have a new independent credit report obtained by them for each loan applicant as required by its lending guidelines. I later learned that Ms. Joiner has been terminated by wholesale mortgage investor #2 and is now working for wholesale mortgage investor #1—again!

In February 2005, I received notification from HUD's Quality Assurance Division of its intention to conduct an on-site review of Primero's Single Family FHA mortgage origination activities, practices and procedures. We fully complied with HUD's request for an on-site inspection and made available our office and all documents requested by HUD. In addition, I spent a great deal of time speaking with the auditors to advise them of the misrepresentations and suspected fraud uncovered.

On May 5, 2005, I met with a Special Agent from HUD's Office of Inspector General and a Senior Special Agent from the Office of Immigration and Customs Enforcement. This meeting lasted for more than two hours and I provided the agents with details concerning the suspected fraudulent activities I uncovered with respect to a significant number of the HUD/FHA loans originated by Primero.

I have provided the agents with key information that will assist them in their ongoing investigation. In addition, I have voluntarily provided the agents with documentation demonstrating the suspected fraud, and made arrangements with the Special Agent to have a forensic computer technician image the computers that Ms. Mead and her assistants used at Primero's office. Both Primero, in general, and myself, in particular, are cooperating fully with this investigation and are willing to provide the agents with any information they need.

After all the work we have done since last year, going through the HUD audit, speaking with investigators, here is how I believe the "mortgage marauders" were able to slip under our radar and work undetected for as long as they did: it all started with a person marketing to first-time home buyers and emerging market borrowers. These populations are vulnerable and often unsophisticated; overwhelmed by the facts and figures and the number of forms they have to fill out to be approved for a loan.

Taking advantage of their vulnerability, the mortgage marauders would promise these people that they could buy a home, with no credit, bad credit or with good credit, whether the paycheck they received showed enough to qualify and whether they had sufficient housing history credit. This person was not a real estate agent but someone who had made a deal with several licensed real estate agents to get a substantial marketing fee for bringing these clients to close a home purchase under them.

As you can imagine, with such skimpy qualifications needed to buy a home, they had buyers lining up around the block. Then, once the false information needed was established for each couple, the real estate people would bring the home buyers to Primero for a loan application.

Ms. Mead and her team would then go to work, alter the credit report, obtain phony alternative credit letters, hire a specific appraiser that was part of the plan, send out a phony verification of rent, and then certify that the documents going to the real estate marketing team were a true copy of the original.

As for the documentation itself, the borrowers would need any or all of the following: phony paycheck stubs, W-2 forms, tax returns, etc. Sometimes the employer never even existed. In such cases, they would have specific telephone numbers being answered by, let's say, ABC Construction and would possibly even register that company with the state, if necessary, to make it seem like a legitimate employer.

A lot of these borrowers turned out to be people that never had a chance to make the payments based on their real jobs and take home pay. They would also have phony landlord information to prove that the borrower had a "great" 12-month rental history. They would obtain fake social security cards, green cards, and even a driver's license if needed.

You are probably starting to get the picture: whatever they needed to help the borrower qualify and get approved, they had a document or system in place to get the loan approved, but they knew how the wholesale investors worked so that is when they must have decided they needed legitimate "inside people" at several more levels of the transaction.

They had underwriters that were overlooking obvious loan conditions or documents. This would have meant the loan would be declined. They had closers involved so that if underwriters would condition for what we call "at closing conditions," it was the closer's job to bring the conditions to the underwriter for review and final approval prior to funding the loan. In our loans the conditions were not provided, thus the closer was not supposed to fund the loan; instead they allowed the loan to fund and close.

I believe the reason this all came to be so easy—and why it is still happening today—is based in large part on FHA 97% financing and the seller-assisted down payment program for the 3% down payment needed and all closing costs, as well as other 100% programs using either 1 loan or 2 loans—called 80/20's.

In such cases, the borrower does not have to invest any of their own money, because these programs allow the seller to pay all the closing costs and prepaid escrow accounts needed to close the loan. These are great loan products for legitimate borrowers that have good credit and jobs that have just never been able to save money for a down payment and closing costs, but also great for the Mortgage Marauders, as they do not have to invest anything but time to commit mortgage fraud.

Why do I mention all this? Why have I laid my soul bare for all to see? Please know that I'm not trying to scare you or paint a picture of the real estate mortgage business that is all doom and gloom. It isn't.

You and I both know that this is a good business, a helpful business, populated by honest, hardworking, professional, and friendly people who do their jobs well and would never even think of breaking the law.

Even after all I've been through I still come to work every day full of hope and progress because of the good people I work with—and for all of the people that deserve to buy a home and need good, honest help in accomplishing the American dream of owing a home.

Truth be told, I am sharing all of this with you as a cautionary tale. I did everything right, and still it wasn't enough. I dotted every "i" and crossed every "t" and still someone found a way to use my good name to do bad business.

My story, in general, and this book, in particular, are designed to arm you with the tools you'll need to combat the forces of those who would commit fraud. These people cared nothing about my company, myself, or the good people they hurt by creating fraudulent loans that lined their pockets and robbed the rest of us of our good names. Their credentials looked great on paper; they talked the talk and even walked the walk, and fooled an experienced business owner who had been in the real estate industry for nearly two decades.

I guess my point is if it can happen to me, it can happen to you.

But it doesn't have to…

Together we can learn what it takes to stop mortgage fraud, not just at our own companies but at every level of the playing field. From the consumer to our loan officers, processors, VPs to our CFOs and to our receptionists, fraud exists—and begins—at every layer and to avoid becoming a victim we must be vigilant about combating fraud at every step.

Together we can do just that.

Let's begin, shall we?

Chapter 1:
Welcome to the Unethical World of Mortgage Fraud (An Overview)

"Appraisal fraud is part of a bigger, more ominous picture. As home prices have continued to increase above inflation…American homeowners are vulnerable as never before to financial ruin if home prices fall to their natural market value…"

~ David Callahan, author of *Home Insecurity: How Widespread Appraisal Fraud Puts Homeowners at Risk*

Would you ever say the "F" word in public? Do you even dare to bring the "F" word up in polite conversation? After all, if you even *mention* the "F" word it makes any honest, hard working real estate professional quiver. The "F" word is a dirty word in the mortgage industry, and for good reason.

So, have you guessed it yet? What, exactly, IS the "F" word?

"Fraud." More specifically: "Mortgage Fraud."

Don't get me wrong: fraud isn't a factor in every mortgage loan, or even in every branch, but the outcome of even one fraudulent loan can affect the entire industry, in general, and individual practitioners, specifically.

The ripple effect of fraud is as deep as it is far-reaching. The mortgage lenders and borrowers stand to lose much more than the cost of the damages when fraud appears. At risk is the lender's reputation in the industry and the borrower's financial well-being. And as all of us know, in THIS industry our word is our bond; our reputation is our bread and butter.

Who of us, after all, can afford to lose that precious commodity?

Where does mortgage fraud begin and how do we prevent—or at least begin to stop—mortgage fraud? They say timing is everything, and in this case there's never been a better time to commit—or fall prey to—mortgage fraud. The unprecedented real estate boom over the last few years has led to the doubly dangerous refinancing craze that swept the nation as a result.

This one-two double-whammy has sucker-punched its share of consumers, resulting in widespread appraisal fraud whereby property values are greatly—and unjustifiably—inflated to prey on the unsophisticated buyer who is then left holding the note on a property worth but a fraction of the value at which it had been improperly appraised.

Of course, that's just what happens on the consumer end. How can we, as practitioners working within the industry, control *our* end of the mortgage fraud equation? Unfortunately, the problem is as internal as it is systemic.

According to Lew Schielman, a popular columnist for www.landlord.com, "For the most part…the perpetrator isn't a professional thief—or even the borrower— it's one or more of the dozen or so specialists—the loan officer, appraiser, real estate agent, title agent—who touches the mortgage as it winds its way through the approval process. Most cases—80 percent by one estimate—involve insiders…"

Is it any wonder? After all, loan originators and their team members have detailed access to the borrower's information in the transaction. From social security numbers to bank account information, it's all above board and on the table. Many of us treat such information as sacrosanct, keeping it under lock and key and using it for one purpose and one purpose only. To those who would perpetrate fraud, however, such information becomes the key they use to unlock the door to fraud.

Every part of the mortgage lending process presents another window of opportunity to unscrupulous loan originators, who by the very nature of their job description come in contact with builders, real estate agents, borrowers, processors, underwriters, appraisers, lender account reps, and title closers. Each one of these positions or areas needed to get a mortgage leaves an opportunity for fraud!

There are two reasons such folks commit fraud:

- **Type # 1:** *Soft Fraud to obtain a property—where someone lies about facts to get a loan to buy a property.*
- **Type # 2:** *Hard Fraud to make an immediate profit—where someone lies about the facts to make a profit.*

We will get into the details of these specific reasons shortly, but for now it's important to know the "why" before we can understand the "how." And, although the reasons people commit fraud are limited, the means by which they go about their dirty business evolves constantly, changing with the whims of the market, the individual, their personality, and most especially the latest technology to which they are privy.

Technology has been one significant reason for the rise in mortgage fraud. The tools that such criminals use are as simple as they are effective: a computer, printers, design software, a little ingenuity, and an unscrupulous individual can have fraudulent loan documents in no time.

From a fictitious appraiser's letterhead to a forged notary seal, today's design software is a veritable candy store to those who would defraud you, your company, or your clients out of their hard-earned money.

Although most people can rise above the temptation of profit ill-gained, our responsibility does not end there. As individuals and as an industry, we need to play an active part in fighting fraud. The days of relying only on the federal government to protect us are over, and to believe in the goodwill of fraudulent practitioners to police themselves is pure folly.

Until we stop fraud on a case-by-case basis, establishing significant penalties and sobering preventative measures, fraud will continue to reach epidemic proportions in our industry. We must be vigilant against fraud, recognizing its signs and taking proactive, definite, and realistic steps to not only prevent it but also punish it.

It starts with me.

It starts with you.

It starts with *us*…

Although we will discuss each of these steps in more detail later, one way in which employers can begin fighting fraud right now, today, is to come up with an incentive program for those employees who report or prevent fraud. Why? The answer is deceptively simple: Because the employees participating with the fraudsters are most likely doing it for profit.

In addition to preventing fraud on an individual mortgage loan, employees and employers have the power to take action on a national level by starting or joining a local or national association working against mortgage fraud. As few of us are political animals, this needs to be fought on a grassroots level for the better of the industry.

Rest assured, the extra work will instill confidence about what type of person you are with you or your employer, builders, real estate agents, borrowers, processors, underwriters, appraisers, lender account reps, title closers and others.

As I stated at the opening of this chapter, nothing is more precious to those of us in this industry than our good reputation; taking positive steps to curb fraud in your own backyard will establish you as an upstanding practitioner in the local real estate community.

Let's be honest: we can't always prevent fraud through proactive measures. While we are busy running our companies or processing loans, fraudsters are spending all their time—and I do mean *all*, as in every waking second—thinking of new, inventive, and difficult to detect ways to do what they do. It's nearly impossible to keep up with such dedicated, aggressive, and workaholic criminals. (If only they would spend the same amount of time on their day job, they'd make enough money to make fraud redundant!)

When we can't prevent fraud, then, we must report it. Although we should do this because it is part of or job—not to mention the *legal* thing to do—we do not always report fraud. Sometimes we feel this will reflect badly upon us; other times we simply don't know who to report the fraud *to*.

We can't turn a blind eye to fraud. Not only does this make us an unknowing accessory when it happens in our own company—on our watch—but it's the very reason fraud remains so rampant. Those who would commit fraud know that few will report it if they're discovered and, even if they do, by then they will have moved on to avoid penalty. The only way to stop such a widespread, global problem is to look ourselves squarely in the mirror and promise to fight fraud wherever, and whenever, we can.

This means not passing the buck. For instance, when management from one company knows that an employee that has just been fired has committed fraud, and then turns them loose into the industry to find another naive company, that former employer needs to have the responsibility—ethically if not legally—for any further fraudulent actions that person may perform if they do not report the fraud.

Here is a prime example: if a real estate agent knows a borrower is planning to buy an investment property but finds out that they checked the box on page 3 of the residential loan application claiming they are going to "owner-occupy" the home, they have a responsibility to inform you about it. Right? It only makes sense that if you know about fraud but do nothing; you are in effect contributing to that fraud. But do they and, if so, what percentage do not? Chances are, the number for the former are low and the latter are high. After all, alerting someone to the oversight may cancel the contract and all the parties mentioned above lose a commission, bonus or incentive of some type from the transaction.

Fighting fraud is hardest when it hits our own wallet…

The management of these companies also share in some of these responsibilities for their employees, preferred partners, and borrowers, and need to set up pre-funding audit procedures to establish that they want to both protect the innocent and scrutinize a random percentage of the mortgage loans prior to the closing and funding of the mortgage to prevent fraud.

The implication here is clear: our industry *has* to implement new training techniques for the people just starting out in the real estate industry. Sadly, however, we seem to be using age-old training methods even though we have new technology—and the Mortgage Marauders always use the latest technology and techniques.

We won't be able to change the industry overnight. It will take time, training, and talent to stem the growing tide of mortgage fraud. We will have to learn and grow, not only professionally but personally as well. The fight will be hard, the battles many, and the road long. But take heart: by picking up this book, you've already taken the first—and possibly hardest—step.

Now I think you're ready for your next one…

Chapter 2:
How to Start Closing the Door on Fraud (Prevention before Detection)

"The number of incidents of mortgage fraud is increasing and the types of incidents are becoming more severe and costly to the (mortgage) industry."
~ **Williams Mathews, the Mortgage Asset Research Institute**

For those who still believe the word "epidemic" is too strong an adjective to describe the occurrence of mortgage fraud in today's real estate industry, they need only look to a flurry of recent headlines to find the proof in the mortgage fraud pudding:

- Federal prosecutors in Denver have broken a mortgage fraud ring that preyed on illegal immigrants. The *Rocky Mountain News* is reporting that a federal grand jury is indicting two on charges of mail and wire fraud, along with witness tampering. They were doing business with first-time home-buyers in Hispanic neighborhoods who were duped into buying homes they couldn't afford by applying for mortgages with phony credit histories, employment information and income statements. They were bribing mortgage company employees to speed up and approve loans; they were also buying cheap homes, making minor improvements and then jacking up the price before selling them to "…unsophisticated, low-income buyers."
- As an employee of a sub prime lending giant, this person had access to the company's computerized application tracking system. That's not all that unusual since she worked as a correspondent service representative and it was her job to screen loan applications, but with a few well-placed key strokes she changed 11 mortgage loans, resulting in the borrowers receiving more money than they were approved to receive. But when the loans defaulted, an anonymous phone call to the company helped federal investigators nail her. She called the scheme "bankruptcy for profit" and said she was receiving kickbacks from mortgage brokers to approve the loans.
- Four real estate agents have pled guilty to felony conspiracy charges in assisting 19 borrowers, who have all admitted making false statements on federal loan documents.

- A husband and wife are going to jail for running a Denver-area mortgage fraud scheme that included greasing a banker with a bribe; they have also been convicted of federal mail and bank fraud. He will do 15 months; she got a year and a day. The hubby must also pay more than $800,000 in restitution. The misdeeds included reportedly altering income statements and appraisals and bribing a bank employee to go along with their scheme. The federal judge handling the case gave the banker three years probation.

- The owners of a home improvement company, a bar, a cellular phone firm, a roofer and a computer company were among the 12 people charged by federal authorities in Illinois with trying to rip off HUD. The "loan scam," as the FBI reportedly described it to television station WREX, involved the ring using fake and forged documents to dupe HUD into making up to $2 million in bad loans. The Ringleader and his wife would allegedly buy cheap houses and then pay $500 to anyone referring a buyer to them. But the buyers couldn't have qualified for the loans, so they allegedly worked along with two others in paying the $500 bounty to businesses that would provide false employment records for the buyers.

- Hispanics targeted in fraud scheme: two Pennsylvania men, a mortgage broker and a real estate agent are going to federal prison for running a predatory lending scam that targeted poor Hispanic immigrants.

- Broker faces prison again: with a prison record because of mortgage fraud, a California man is accused of using a stolen identification to illegally broker loans.

- Man will do a year behind bars for using a friend's identity to buy two homes.

- Five men in the Pittsburgh area have been indicted by a federal grand jury for running an alleged fraud ring that targeted poor neighborhoods and resulted in $1.8 million in phony loans. More than 20 properties were involved. The "straw buyers" were given kickbacks for allowing their identities to be used.

- A Michigan Mortgage Company's direct mail ad solicitation touched off a mini-panic among some Tampa, Florida and area homeowners who were told they were behind on their taxes. The company was trying to get homeowners to refinance to payoff the taxes.

- A closing agent pleaded guilty to federal charges of conspiring to defraud mortgage lenders and the U.S. Department of Housing and Urban Development, or HUD. Prosecutors allege while working for various title companies, the agent was not collecting the funds she was supposed to during real estate transactions. She was working with the co-defendants in the case; a real estate investor and speculator who were allegedly selling newly purchased houses at inflated prices—the illegal process known as "flipping."

- The owner of a failed St. Louis area title company is looking at the possibility of jail time for allegedly running a nearly $4 million mortgage scam. The feds say he cleaned out $3.84 million in escrow funds he was supposed to be holding for customers.
- "He" was buying the house of his dreams, a $4.9 million mansion that included a guesthouse in Bergen County, N.J. Only he didn't exist. He was made up by a man who has pleaded guilty to numerous state charges of insurance and mortgage fraud, according to information from the New Jersey Attorney General's office. The real man created the fake borrower, along with fake promissory notes and financial statements, to entice a mortgage lender to make a loan on the property. The money, of course, went to a real man, prosecutors charged. A mortgage broker in Arkansas got stuck with the phony promissory note after buying it from the original mortgage lender.
- A broker in Longmont, Colorado is accused of stealing a client's identity and then using the bogus persona to take an $8,000 Caribbean cruise and run up $40,000 in credit card debt. She was arrested and charged with using a client's Social Security number to open at least two bank accounts. When arrested she was an escrow manager for a title company. But police believe her alleged thefts were orchestrated while working at a mortgage company, which is apparently out of business.
- A North Carolina real estate lawyer and two business associates have been arrested for operating a mortgage fraud ring that used "double closings" to make money.
- An alleged mortgage fraud ring operating out of Houston offered up a $5,000 bounty for houses that could be used in the scheme. Prosecutors say the ring paid $5,000 to the buyers of 12 homes. The buyers then helped in the fraud by allowing their homes to be used in the scheme, which included falsely inflating the incomes and work histories of buyers; creating false documents; making false statements to lenders; making up references; and telling lenders they were going to live in the houses when the sales were completed.

*[**Source:** I have found, read, and used information about these articles at*
www.mortgagedaily.com]

As one can clearly see from this tidal wave of recent headlines (which themselves represent just the *tip* of the iceberg), mortgage fraud is "persistent and growing." While it may seem too big to curtail on our own, try to stop it we must. In this case, prevention begins not with millions, not with thousands, not with hundreds, but with one: one loan officer, one loan office, one mortgage company, one credit reporting agency—one person—at a time.

As an industry we need to strengthen our pre-funding controls by training loan officers—as well as processors, underwriters, the closing departments and a host of collateral employees who likewise have their fingers on the process—how to better detect fraudulent loan applications and real estate transactions.

Most authorities will agree that the most effective method in preventing mortgage fraud is consistent regulation and licensing enforced by the appropriate authorities, but if your state does not have strong regulations or laws, you need to rely on a strong in-house, company quality control plan that includes both pre- and post-closing loans.

After all, it is your business or income whether you are an owner, loan officer processor or being paid to be involved in the transaction. Without proper enforcement, current regulations are of almost no consequence. The latest industry statistics state that in 2004 there were over 17,000 reports of "suspicious activities" filed within the mortgage industry, and of those only about two percent—that's no typo, a measly 2 %—were ever investigated.

No wonder the fraudsters don't fear retribution!

However, the tide is slowly changing…

There's a story often told about a solitary man out taking a stroll on the beach. Eventually he comes upon a portion of the beach where millions of dying starfish have been washed upon the shore by an unusually high tide. The man is shocked by the sheer number of starfish and how many will perish because of Mother Nature's folly.

As he continues walking he sees more and more starfish stretching as far as the eye can see. Step by step he becomes more convinced of the futility of it all. He begins to question his own mortality, and wonders if he and his vain attempts to find meaning in life aren't a lot like all those starfish; washed upon the shore and destined for a slow, painful death.

Finally he comes across a little boy who, much like himself, is confronted with the massive proportions of those millions of dying starfish. The two stand side by side, silently contemplating the holocaust. Finally, the boy reaches down to pick up a single starfish, flinging it out to sea.

The man snorts and says, "Why bother? You'll never save them all. How can you possibly make a difference?"

The boy shrugs, reaches down to grab up another starfish and, before flinging it out to sea says, "I can make a difference to *this* starfish." Struck by the significance—not to mention the simplicity—of this statement, the man too reaches down to begin flinging starfish back into the sea, one by one.

Let us be like these two brave souls; not intimidated by the futility of facing fraud in our industry, but hearty enough to begin making a change in our own backyard, fighting fraudsters—one by one.

Notice the Warning Signs of Fraud

Part of the reason so few fraudsters are caught is because we fail to recognize the warning signs of fraud. I choose to believe that the main reason we don't spot fraud is because of our ignorance, not our negligence.

I have personally learned many of the warning signs of fraud, but only *after* HUD had stopped allowing us to obtain FHA case numbers for new loan originations and threatened to do so indefinitely.

Remember: Loan fraud is typically committed with intent; it is not normally requested or asked for by the home buyer, but by the originator or real estate professional, or both in partnership in order for the loan to close so the originator and real estate agent can make a profit. To spare you that kind of distress, I share with you now the following warning signs of fraud:

- **Information that looks false, inflated or "too good to be true" (that usually means it is);**
- **Variations in a person's signature on the same application (or other possible signs of forgery);**
- **Missing information that's promised at a later date, such as forgetting the proper ID's for the Patriot Act...**

To better detect such signs of fraud you should use what I call a pre-funding warning system, which includes documents or items in the file that warrant questions. These are questions that must be addressed prior to funding a loan, they are not always fraud related, and sometimes one document leads to the need of another document to explain the red flag.

I list these warning signs because having experienced fraud on a personal level, only after it was too late to do anything about it, I firmly believe that prevention is the key to finding a cure for this industry-wide "disease." If we can spot the warning signs and stop a fraudulent mortgage loan *before* it goes through, we are halfway to beating the fraudsters at their own game.

In his cautionary article entitled "How to Commit Loan Fraud," Jonathan A. Goodman explains: "Lenders tend not to notice loan fraud unless the loan goes into default. Over the last decade or so we have had a strong real estate economy. Appreciation tends to cover up loan fraud. But declining property values have begun to reveal problems. People in the real estate industry should be especially vigilant to avoid misleading mortgage investors about the true price which the buyer pays for the property."

In a white paper article on mortgage fraud author Patrick Crowley explains, "Many law enforcement officials, mortgage lenders, industry experts, security companies and others agree that the best way to fight fraud is a multi-tiered approach that includes cooperation between the industry and law enforcement, quality control measures enhanced through technology, a better method to report mortgage fraud and tougher laws."

As specified, one part of this "multi-tiered approach" begins with us. We as an industry need to step up our own brand of self-enforcement. How? Simple: by appointing a specific person within each branch as a contact within your company, reporting directly to senior management what they themselves find or what they are told by employees concerning possibly fraudulent loan files.

That person needs to be informed about current fraud schemes or issues within that market and, to assure that happens, upper management needs to invest in that person's education to fight fraud. As I've since found there are many ways in which to learn about this subject, through various seminars, courses, and consultants, but often companies have not been or are not now willing to spend the money to do so. They *have* started to use on-line services to verify certain information, but have not done a very good job of training their people, who are ordering this information on how spot the red flags. I can't stress enough how much an investment in training like this can save you tenfold in the long run.

All parties to the mortgage transaction should have a "go to" guy or gal firmly established in each branch. This becomes the single person to contact when they suspect fraud, without having to fear the act of vengeance from the fraudster themselves. It is vital that reporting fraud be a pain-, hassle-, and result-free experience or even those employees with the best of intentions simply won't do it.

We also need help tracking the loan with the payment servicing mortgage companies. After all, they know the most about a loan's history and, furthermore, have the ability to identify the common factors or individuals in all of the mortgage transactions. Now, even though this is post-closing fraud prevention it could also assist in pre-funding fraud schemes at a local level; the main point here is the importance of information sharing.

The U.S. Patriot Act allows information sharing about financial matters involving suspected money launderers or terrorists to be distributed to financial institutions. Sadly, the mortgage industry has not (yet) learned how to use the Patriot Act appropriately or to its advantage.

This measure may not prevent all fraud, but it could help prevent large losses that occur as a result of fraud. On a smaller scale, reporting fraud is the first step to eliminating it from our industry.

First Identify It; Then Report It:
How (and Where) to Report Suspected Fraud

I realize that this information is all well and good, but sometimes we can put the cart before the horse and as a result all we get is nowhere fast. In other words, it does us no good to be told to report fraud if we don't know *where* to report fraud. Well, I'm here to put that question to rest. (With a little help from my friends at the MBA and HUD-OIG, that is.)

The first place to report fraud is at the local level. Every state has its own reporting agency, but where to find it? Fortunately, the helpful folks at the Mortgage Bankers Association, or MBA, have set up a database of such agencies at their website, www.stopmortgagefraud.com.

This is the consumer-reporting site posted by the MBA. As the MBA explains, "This online resource is designed to be a one-stop shop for the industry to gather the information tools they need to combat this problem." Among the frequently updated fraud alerts and up-to-the-minute news about fraud posted there, the site also includes a popular and easy-to-use resource library.

For your convenience, here is the helpful contact information I've tracked down for you that our industry needs to make known at every level:

> The Office of Inspector General is the department that investigates loan fraud for HUD and all lenders should report any fraud to, at the very least:
> www.hotline@hudoig.gov
>   HUD-OIG Hotline: 1-800-347-3735
>   Fax-202-708-4829
>   400 Virginia Ave., Suite C-120, SW
>   Washington, DC 20024

Best of all, however, might be the access the sites afford you to local resources that can be very helpful to you on a personal—and professional—level. To contact your state agency, for instance, you can simply type in your 5-digit zip code and, in the blink of an eye, discover the contact information you need to report fraud.

Sound simple? It is.

Sometimes, doing the right thing *can* be simple.

So, what are you waiting for?

I'll Get By
(With a Little Help From My Friends)

To ensure that Primero's loan files would be vigorously reviewed and audited, Primero terminated its quality assurance program with Quality R US and retained the services of Dr. Gary Lacefield, with the Risk Mitigation Group. Dr. Lacefield was a Senior Rights Analyst, Investigator, and Supervisor of Lending Investigations for none other than HUD.

Dr. Lacefield has been advised of the misrepresentations and suspected fraudulent activities uncovered by Primero and is vigilantly reviewing Primero's loan files to ensure regulatory compliance and monitoring its default status with HUD.

Why go to such extremes? Well, I believe that it is critical to have a totally up to date and knowledgeable quality control company and plan in place. After all, during our audit with HUD we were written up for having a sub-standard quality control plan.

Upon learning of the default status, Primero has taken great efforts to mitigate these losses. I was mortified that some of our clients had been on the receiving end of fraud without even knowing about it, but also mortified that some *did* know about what had happened to get the mortgage approved. Now I could truly feel how the innocent felt, and it spurred me to undertake a number of initiatives to ease their pain and suffering including, but not limited, to:

- Mailing a letter to borrowers in default advising of this status and requesting a meeting;
- Visiting borrowers' homes to speak with them personally about the matter;
- Meeting with borrowers to discuss default status on their loans;
- Assisting borrowers with completing financial worksheet for default payment program;
- Assisting borrower with locating a realtor to sell their home;
- Mailing payments for borrowers via FedEx, Airborne Express, or Western Union;
- Making telephone calls to borrowers and the investor regarding default status; and
- Assisting borrowers with repayment plan...

As a result, I am happy to report that more than twenty of the loans identified by HUD as being in default are no longer in default status. In addition to mitigating current defaults, Primero has reinforced with all future borrowers the importance of timely payment of their mortgages and staying out of default. All borrowers are advised to contact Primero in the event that they have questions regarding their mortgages or problems making payments.

In addition, we also mail out letters as a friendly reminder for the first 3 months—in both English and Spanish—that their house payment is now due; sometimes payments are missed in the first three months due to the way our industry sells and transfers the loans in those first 90 days.

How I Fought Back:
An Action Plan

When I received that devastating letter from HUD, my whole life changed, not just professionally but personally as well. I realized that my business and my life were forever intertwined. The betrayal, the shame, the accusations hit home on a basic level that colored everything I did, said, or promised from that day forward.

Through the help of several licensed professionals in our industry I completely revamped our company's "game plan," as it were, for preventing, identifying, and reporting fraud. First I came up with a complete Quality Control Plan that HUD approved of during the Audit (as the plan I had in place was considered "insufficient" by the HUD auditors). I did some of this with the help of Dr. Lacefield. The Quality Control Plan states, among other things:

> "...Primero Home Loan will report any material violation of law or regulation, material false statement or program abuse by Primero, its employees or any other party to the transaction to the appropriate Agency office. Primero Home Loan will furnish Audit findings regarding an Agency's loans to that Agency on demand. Where required by Freddie Mac, Fannie Mae, FHA or any other agency Primero will also provide Audit reports to the investors for loans if requested by those Investors..."

Furthermore, every loan officer, loan coordinator, or loan processor signs the Quality Control Plan before they ever log a single hour working for my company. Not only does this signed, legal document distance me from various liability issues resulting from the employee's actions, but I feel it's a strong deterrent to acting improperly in the first place.

Remember, fraud often starts small. A fudged figure here, an incomplete loan application there, an over-generous appraisal, but little do employees know that these "little lies" are actually fraudulent information and, in fact, possibly criminal. To prevent such temptations, this document states such information at the outset of their employment.

Another document I developed to combat fraud in our industry, in general, and our company, in particular, is entitled "Loan Officer Responsibilities and Guidelines." This 10-page document lays out, step-by-step, the loan officer's responsibilities and reminds them to be ever vigilant of fraud throughout the entire process.

The piece de resistance in this process is a document entitled Loan Fraud: Zero Tolerance Statement. In no uncertain terms, the document begins with an all-out declaration about how I feel about fraud:

> *"All Primero loan officers, loan officer assistants and processors must be aware that they bear the responsibility of all incidents of fraud for loans originated by Primero Home Loan. The loan officer, loan officer assistant, and/or processor are responsible for the content and quality of each application taken and each loan submitted to our investors. THE SUBMISSION OF A LOAN APPLICATION CONTAINING FALSE INFORMATION IS A CRIME!"*

This last warning, I think, can never be stressed too often or, for that matter, too harshly: *THE SUBMISSION OF A LOAN APPLICATION CONTAINING FALSE INFORMATION IS A CRIME!*

We've talked about how common loan fraud is, discussed the statistics, heard from the experts, but I think what's been missing so far in our discussion has been an examination of the people who actually commit fraud. We'll get a little more deeply into this in future chapters but for now it's just important to note that institutions don't commit fraud, lenders don't commit fraud, companies don't commit fraud—*people* commit fraud.

On an individual level, each of us has the power to resist doing something illegal. And never forget, that's what we're talking about here. Hands down, no bones about it, fraud is an illegal act perpetrated by individuals. The power of these audits and reviews is that they make the individual who might be tempted to commit fraud pause, even if just for a minute, and gives him or her time to change the course of action.

Don't get me wrong: The level of pre-funding audits and review do not replace fraud investigations. However, if done right and done often, they can prevent the reason for the investigation in the first place. I know, I know: all of this—the time to write the documents, edit them, print them, reproduce them, even enforce them—means more time and money out of your pocket.

However, please do not let the additional time and expenses required to implement such a plan stop you from having a detailed pre-funding plan. To prove to you just how valuable they are, consider:

- **It is too late to prevent fraud after closing:** Because the damage is already done and you can't go back and make changes to a loan *after* the fact;

- **The civil and criminal penalties...**for non-compliance in reporting fraud relating to the Patriot Act or HUD regulations could come back to haunt you if you don't take proper steps to prevent, report, and stop fraud;
- **The internal cost of a fraudulent mortgage:** is an area that most lenders have trouble calculating but consider that the rehiring cost, reputation cost, lost loans from HUD cost, etc., are much more devastating than the comparatively insignificant costs of reproducing materials for audits and reviews;
- **The external cost of a fraudulent mortgage...**is directly related to the actual money lost in association with a fraudulent loan, such as repurchase, foreclosure, etc.

These steps may sound severe but anything I can do to avoid fraud, I believe, is a step in the right direction. It is my firm belief that if every company used these documents, or some variation thereof, those who would commit fraud would at least think twice before doing so, and possibly be caught along the way if they did decide to do so thanks to all the stop-gap measures inherent in their design.

We've learned what fraud is and why experts agree that it's currently reaching epidemic proportions. Now I think it's time to begin learning how to spot the signs of fraud and, hopefully, prevent my professional and personal nightmare from ever happening to you. We'll start with noting some red flags that may alert you to potentially fraudulent activities.

Chapter 3:
Stopping the Paper Trail—Where Fraud Originates

"The potential impact of mortgage fraud on financial institutions and the stock market is clear. If fraudulent practices become systemic within the mortgage industry and mortgage fraud is allowed to become unrestrained, it will ultimately place financial institutions at risk and have adverse effects on the stock market..."

~ Chris Swecker, assistant director of the FBI's Criminal Investigative Division

One of the most difficult aspects of dealing with mortgage fraud is that it's hard to know the scope of the problem. The human element that's involved makes would-be fraudsters hard to spot, and those already committing fraud even harder to identify. Because these people are white-collar criminals, they look, dress, act, and talk just like the rest of us. They won't look like criminals; they'll look like loan officers, real estate agents, members of management and loan processors or closers and, of course, the girl or boy next door.

Whether it's in our own company or simply a scourge of the industry itself, fraud is rampant, invasive, and ever present. Here are just some of the ways in which fraud is perpetrated:

- Loan application fraud;
- Exaggerated appraisals;
- Falsified or fake credit reports;
- Falsified housing history;
- Falsified income;
- Forged tax returns;
- Fake title insurance;
- Fake Social Security Numbers...

Worse than the many ways in which fraud can be committed, though, are the many people *tempted* to commit it. They don't just look and dress like us, they *are* us. They smile at you every morning in the office break room, dance with you at the Christmas party, and sign the inter-office greeting card on your birthday.

How did this happen to our industry? Who is doing this to our companies? Why are federal institutions and governmental agencies getting involved? Where will it end and will the typical borrower ever feel confident in the mortgage loan industry again? For that matter, can we ever feel confident in *ourselves* again?

While these are good questions all, many of these issues are better left to the powers that be. We can talk history and philosophy and the decency of man until we're blue in the face, but that's not what you're here for, now is it? You are here for action; you are here for results.

The action?

Vigilance. Prevention. Reportage. Apprehension…

The results?

A company devoid of fraud or, at the very least, a company that's pro-active against fraud and no longer willing to turn a blind eye to those who would commit illegal activity on our watch.

Well, get ready to "kick it up a notch," as they say in the food industry, because here are some actual red flags you can start looking for right now, today.

Don't worry; if they don't sink in at first, on my website I have a whole section on red flags for employment, credit reports, self-employed, and appraisals used in my training classes. There you can find much of the following information in one form or another. Before we get to the red flags I want you to remember two very important caveats:

1.   Does the information in the file make sense?

It's important to take all of this information with a grain of salt and, once you finish this book, close it, and walk away you'll be left with only your good, common sense. That common sense should tell you that fraudulent files often "feel" fraudulent, even if you don't know what you're looking for.

After all, you won't necessarily start spotting more fraudulent files because there are more; you'll start spotting them more because you know better now. The bullet points to follow contain specific red flags, but in general you should begin to acquire a better sense of what feels wrong, in general, about a fraudulent file. Armed with that knowledge, you can then check off the following lists until you find the actual red flag that caused you concern in the first place.

2.   Not every red flag contains fraud!

Let's not go on a witch hunt here. By no means am I implying that every individual you run across intends to commit fraud, nor is every file you encounter likely to be fraudulent. As you and I both know, our industry is full of talented, ethical, and professional individuals who would never stoop to such a level.

However, the threat exists and that's why I introduce these red flags here for you now. I just wanted to remind you how easy it is to get caught up in the pervading sense of paranoia, fear, and distrust that those who would commit fraud unwittingly create. They don't just commit fraud; they infect an entire organization with a lack of trust that is very, very hard to regain. Like someone once said, "You can't un-ring a bell."

When it comes to fraudulent loans, we will be discussing the areas of origin from which fraud may or may not originate, those being:

- **Applicants with an employer (company, government, etc.)**
- **Applicants who are self-employed**
- **Social Security Number identity theft or fraud**
- **The details about the property in question**

Now, with all of the above being taken into consideration, here are the red flags to look for in your loan packages:

Red Flags for Employment

- Evidence of "white-outs" or alterations on VOE, pay stub and/or W-2;
- "Squeezed-in" numbers, i.e. a number being added to a space too small for it;
- Appearance that verification of employment form was hand-carried instead of mailed—i.e. the document is not folded;
- Rounded dollar amounts on VOE, pay stub and/or W-2;
- Employer's address shown only as a post office box;
- Handwritten pay stubs or W-2 forms;
- Income out of line with type of employment;
- Prepared/signed by originator on the same date as completed/signed by employer;
- VOE contains incorrect spellings;
- Current and prior employment overlaps;
- Date of hire is weekend or holiday (per perpetual calendar);
- Income is primarily commissions or consulting fees (self-employed);
- Borrower is a professional employee but not registered/licensed;
- Illegible signature with no further documentation;
- Inappropriate verification source (secretary, relative, etc.);
- Overtime equals or exceeds base pay;
- Business entity not registered or in good standing with the applicable regulatory agencies;
- No prior years' earnings on VOE;
- Answering machine or answering service at place of business (unless self-employed);
- Type or handwriting identical throughout form;
- Company name and/or employer name are not imprinted on pay stub;
- Social security number not imprinted on pay stub;
- Inconsistent check numbers and or dates on pay stubs;
- Type same throughout document and/or inconsistent;
- Numbers are not aligned on pay stub;
- Check stubs from a large employer are not preprinted;
- Sequence of payroll check numbers do not correspond with the payroll dates;
- Social security number is not consistent on pay stub with loan application;

- FICA amounts are incorrect;
- W-2 contains invalid employer identification number;
- FICA wages/taxes and local taxes (if applicable) exceed ceilings/set percentage on W-2s;
- W-2 copy submitted in file is not "Employee's Copy" (Copy C);
- W-2 contains different type within the form...

As you can see, the list is fairly thorough. Any or all of the above items can point to fraud. I recommend using the above, and the following, lists and posting them somewhere prominently. Also, share it with those employees charged with conducting internal audits.

We've seen what to look for in loans originating with employees of one company or another, but another source of fraudulent loan applications comes from those who are self-employed or "other." If you make all borrowers sign a 4506-T at the loan application and inform them that your company will check your income information if your file is chosen for pre-funding quality control, the fraudster most likely will not complete the transaction "as is" with you—and this may even help deter some fraud upfront.

Here is what to be on the lookout for in those cases:

Red Flags for Self-Employed Borrowers

- Tax returns not signed or dated by borrower;
- Evidence of "white-outs" or alterations;
- Borrower with substantial cash in bank reporting little or no interest income;
- Real estate taxes or mortgage interest paid, but no ownership of real property reported (or vice versa);
- Different handwriting or type style within one document;
- Tax computations do not agree with tax tables;
- Address and/or profession does not agree with other information submitted on the loan application;
- No estimated tax payments by self-employed borrower (Schedule SE required);
- Paid preparer signs taxpayer's copy;
- Borrower files Schedule G (income averaging), which is for taxpayers with fluctuating income from year to year;
- Type or handwriting varies within return;
- Higher income borrower does not use a professional tax preparer;
- Schedule A—few or no deductions for high-income taxpayers;
- Schedule A—income deductions listed in round dollar amounts;
- Schedule B—amount or source of income does not agree with the information on loan application;
- Schedule B—no dividends earned on stocks owned;
- Schedule B—borrower with substantial cash in bank shows little or no related interest income;
- Schedule C—borrower shows interest expense but no related loan (business loans with personal liability);
- Schedule C—no "cost of goods sold" on retail or similar operations;
- Schedule E—net income from rents plus depreciation does not equal cash flow as submitted by borrower;
- Schedule E—additional properties listed but not shown on loan application;
- Schedule E—borrower shows partnership income (may be liable as a general partner for partnerships owned)…

Part of my intention for sharing these lists with you is for informational purposes, certainly. However, another part is to express to you—through the enormity of both lists combined—just how many opportunities there are to commit fraud.

This could explain how easy it is to commit and, at the same time, how difficult it is to detect. With all that we have to do in a busy day at the office, how are we ever supposed to catch all of these intricate, complicated facets of an already intricate and complicated loan application?

I'm not suggesting it will happen overnight. Even with all that's happened to me, it's still a challenge to check everything, all the time. But then, it's not supposed to be a solitary, isolated situation. This is a team effort, and by now you can see that it will take all of you—your whole office, our whole industry—to keep the fraudsters in check. Also, over time, it will become a learned process. You will start referring to the checklists less and less and spotting these red flags with your own eyes more and more. It becomes instinct, like tying your shoe or stopping at a red light.

It may seem daunting at first, but it will get easier, trust me…

Now, onto another area that's ripe with opportunity for cunning fraudsters:

Social Security Number Identity Theft or Fraud

While few future homeowners would dare to use their social security number for little more than tax or identification purposes, to the Mortgage Marauders the social security number is one of the main tools in their tool box. Here are some signs that someone may be using a false or invalid social security number to help them commit fraud:

- Is it a valid number issued by the Social Security Administration?
- How many different variations of the number are on credit report?
- Does it match in all areas of the file?
- Is the issued number consistent with the age of the borrower?

Where Bad Social Security Numbers Come From:

- Transpose the numbers, intentionally or not;
- Use a deceased person's number;
- Use children's or a minor's social security number;
- Use a Tax ID number…

And Finally...Property:
Value...there...not there?

In our line of work, the subject property can never be overlooked. We must be constantly vigilant in not only spotting these red flags but also reporting them. We owe it to our company, our industry, our employees, our colleagues, our lenders, our customers, and more importantly, ourselves.

Warning signs that the property itself may be a key player in the fraud to be committed include any or all of the following red flags:

- Comparable properties not verified as recorded (data source MLS, sales office, SREA, CMDC, real estate agent, etc.);
- Tenant shown to be occupant on owner-occupant on refinance application;
- Information blank—borrower, client, occupant, etc.
- Ordered by a party to the transaction other than the originator (i.e. seller, buyer, real estate broker, etc.);
- Tenant shown to be occupant on owner-occupied loan;
- Income approach not used on tenant occupied single-family residences;
- Subject photographs not consistent with date of appraisal or other information contained within the report;
- Photos do not match the description of the house;
- Property Appreciation is shown in a stable or declining market;
- Occupants are unknown;
- Photos reflect a "for sale" sign in refinance loans or "for rent" sign on owner-occupied homes;
- Large "fluff" adjustments (i.e. site, view, etc)...

Pre-Funding Auditing:
Why, When & How?

One of the newest ways to help prevent fraud comes from automated fraud prevention tools, such as various stopgap measures including those forms I've provided for you in the back of this book, on my website, or various software designed to catch suspicious or questionable data.

Now, while we would all agree it is a great start to use these tools, please do not let the technology replace the human factor, because using the online tools could give you a false sense of security. In my opinion, you cannot eliminate the proper on site training of your staff. The best pre-funding technique is a combination of human intervention along with the automated prevention tools. Naturally, I am going to provide the latest list of the online fraud prevention tools available in the appendix, as well as on my website.

I have always given the individuals I work with my total trust until they prove to me otherwise, so basically I believe that people want to do their job and do what it takes to do it right. I don't think I'm alone in this; my employees are well-trained and well-educated mortgage professionals put in place to stop the fraudsters before the loan is funded. Instigating the following pre-funding audit atmosphere in our own workplaces will begin to stop fraud before it is committed, no matter whether it is being done by insiders or others.

Why Do Pre-funding Audits?

There are a variety of reasons to do pre-funding audits, and despite the costs involved in implementing such a program, you will see that the benefits far outweigh the price. Here are just some of the reasons to do pre-funding audits:

- You will stop fraud before the loan closes.
- When you start pre-funding audits you will do the following:
  o Maintain a steady flow of quality originations and closings.
  o Deliver better quality loans to your investors.
  o Your loans will perform better.

- You always need to monitor:
  o Quality of originators, underwriters and third party vendors prior to funding.
  o Information resources for the originator, processor and underwriter to complete the approval decision.
  o Fraud schemes throughout the regional area for loans being originated

Most Crucial Items to Review in Pre-Funding Loan Audits:

- Identification of borrower;
- Knowing your loan officer or who is setting up loan file;
- 1008 and 1003—accuracy;
- Good faith estimate and truth in lending;
- Employment verifications;
- Housing history;
- Credit report;
- Asset verification;
- The real estate contract;
- Preliminary title report;
- Appraisal…

Identification of Borrower(s):
How the Patriot Act Can (and Should) Help YOU

The Patriot Act was written with the intent to battle terrorism, yet it has several provisions that should be helping in the battle against mortgage fraud:

- Section 314-b of the law should benefit mortgage fraud prevention as it provides information sharing among parties involved in the real estate mortgage transaction;
- The Patriot Act law helps us to "know who we are doing business with";
- Identifies clients properly within the guidelines of the Patriot Act for loan being requested, most originators do not know how and what to do with disclosures;
- Lenders need to re-look at the Patriot Act; they will see that it is easy to comply with, all the while helping them know who they are funding a loan for and allowing for information sharing with each other against those who commit fraud with protection from the Patriot Act. (Remember: Legal advice should be obtained in this area on exactly how to use the Patriot Act for information sharing that is best for your company.)

Who is Setting Up the Loan files for Fraud?

- The roles vary depending on the scheme.
- Who targets the borrower or borrower information?
- Who creates the fraudulent loan file?
- Who types in the1003 and disclosures?
- Who is pulling the credit report?
- Who does the verifications: deposits, employment, housing history, etc.?
- Who should inform applicants that any attempt to mislead the lender of any piece of information is fraud and can result in prosecution or calling the loan due and payable—or both?

Closing the Door on Fraud:
Pre-funding Techniques to Prevent Fraud

I have found that the more committed I am in conducting pre-funding audits the more vigilant my employees become in self-policing their own loans. This is a long, challenging process, but one that, given the proper techniques, can begin to work almost immediately. Here are some of the main topics involved in this process.

Pre-funding audits should:

- Research to reveal whether borrower is employed as they represented.
- Will verify the depository information represented.
- Conducting an asset search will reveal public record history and transactions.
- Verifying occupancy by performing an onsite inspection or obtain a utility verification.
- Obtaining licensing, and corporate records to verify information represented.

Knowing your loan officer, broker, processor or anyone involved in reviewing or handling confidential borrower information:

- Has the broker or mortgage company done an exhaustive background check on all parties?
- Is the loan officer listed on the broker approval package?
- Do you get updated info quarterly on the mortgage broker or originator?
- Are there any questionable issues on previous files from this loan officer, broker or processor?
- Are individual underwriters or closers performing services for the same loan officer every time?
- Does the loan officer provide every new file with the same real estate agent?

Critical Red Flag items
help answer critical underwriting questions:

- Is the verification of deposit falsified?
- Is the borrower disclosing all property owned or other potential debt?
- Is the borrower actually self-employed?
- Is the borrower still employed?
- Is the appraisal valid, did the appraiser use good comparables?

Accuracy on the 1008 & 1003:

- Review original application vs. final for large changes or discrepancy:
  - o **Page 1**—Do all of the address and employment information match verifications and identification?
  - o **Page 2**—Are all assets and debts accurate based on verifications?
  - o **Page 3**—Do all the statements made agree with identification?
  - o **Page 4**—Did the borrower(s) sign page 4? Even if blank, but should have an X crossed through the blank area.
  - o Are all the dates on the original documents in compliance with RESPA?
  - o Do all the signatures match on both the original and final documents?
  - o Watch for any signs that the loan has been transferred from another lender.

Good Faith Estimate, Truth in Lending and other Disclosures

- Review original vs. final:
  - o Did fees and charges change radically?
  - o Was the box checked for pre-pay penalty properly on both copies of the TIL?
  - o Are all the dates on the original documents in compliance with RESPA?
  - o Do all the signatures match on both the original and final documents?

Employment & Income Verifications

- Make sure the correct person fills out the VOE at the employer, so when you do the verbal verification it will be re-verified correctly.
- W-2, 1099, Self Employed? Perform a 4506 at the processing level so you do not delay a closing.
- If you use a separate authorization to release information, you should include—in bold type just above the signature line—a statement that although the broker is preparing documents, the loan applicants will be responsible for the accuracy of the information or by creating a separate disclosure for the borrower to sign.

Housing History

- Confirm whether it is a
- private, individual landlord or professional management company.
- Use a separate disclosure (in bold type) with a statement that although the broker is preparing documents, the landlord and the loan applicants will be responsible for the accuracy of the information for the borrower and landlord to sign.

- Copies of checks or money orders: Have the borrower provide copies of the last two months of rent paid based on what they are using.
- Have the credit reporting agency do the third party verification and list on credit report for the source of housing history

Credit Report

- Compare credit report to debts on the 1003 application.
- Review credit scores versus payment history.
- Pull random, if not all new, Q.C. credit report to compare.
- Verify the
- Alternative Credit letters:
  - o Have a list of what type of letters are accepted.
  - o Have the credit reporting agency do a third party verification and list on credit report.

Fannie Mae VOD (Form 1006)

- Bank accounts: Be sure the correct person or department fills out the verification of accounts, current balances, average balances and date opened and signs the document.
- Mattress money: Have the borrower sign the budget letter and use a separate disclosure (in bold type) with a statement that although the broker is preparing documents, the budget letter and the loan applicants will be responsible for the accuracy of the information provided by the borrower.
- A false VOD would be grounds for a repurchase of the loan and reporting of mortgage fraud.
- Request more information on other assets, cars, household assets, etc.: Do they coincide with the assets, income or other statements made on loan application?

The Real Estate Contract

- Review contract and all amend/extends.
- All changes or amend/extends should be signed prior to final approval.
- How many times has the contract been amended or extended?
- Perform random information audits of real estate agents involved in transaction with licensing entity in each state for complaints and to make sure they are actually licensed.

Preliminary Title Report

- Ask for minimum six month chain of title with all submissions.
- Ask for closing protection letter prior to docs.
- Ask for double proof of earnest money deposit:
  1. Proof from borrower
  2. Proof from closing agent

Escrow and Closing Agents

It seems that this part of the transaction appears to be small or even insignificant, but in point of fact it is not. Even matters such as escrow and closing costs can give fraudsters opportunity:

- When reviewing or talking to the service provided by escrow services, settlement-agents or closers they may state their role is limited to just collecting signatures, checking identification, collecting documents or taxes during the closing.
- The actual knowledge the agents have at the closing table is important to stopping or proving fraudulent transactions, i.e. proper identification.
- These agents are the last defense in stopping a fraudulent transaction where the flip occurs. The instruction given to these service providers, in the escrow instructions or settlement instructions or a closing protection letter, can be a stop-gap for fraud prevention and prosecution.

Focus on the Critical Closing Issues:

- The settlement agent should sign not only the HUD-1, but also sign a statement that requires the closing agent to acknowledge the specific closing instructions and that they read, understand, and accept all conditions of conducting the settlement and closing.
- All funds should pass through escrow; this will decrease the potential for down payment frauds, silent seconds, and more. Copies of down payment checks or funds needed to close should be part of the conditions to close; many closers seem to forget this in the closing package.
- All closing instructions and protection letters should contain language stating that the agent acknowledges that there have been no known transfers of the property within the last 60 days and that there have been no significant or material changes in the sales price.
- Borrowers should sign an affidavit at closing stating that they have reviewed all verification documents used in processing the loan and certify that the information in the verifications is accurate.
- All closing instructions should have a due date for returning recorded documents and the final title policy. Sometimes a delay is a red flag for potential fraud; especially property flipping, where the final title policies and/or the recorded deed of trust or mortgage are never delivered. Your closing instructions to the closing agent should include a statement to the effect that, "Failure to return these documents in a timely manner could result in a claim being filed with the title insurer…"
- These four items can be quickly implemented, and could substantially reduce the number of fraudulent loans actually closing. The Closing Instructions worksheet is one of the most important forms for protection against fraud and misrepresentation.

The appraiser is the most essential person in the transaction for cash out, property flipping or other schemes need by the Mortgage Marauders:

- In most mortgage fraud schemes the appraiser must appraise properties in excess of value; otherwise, there is no profit for the fraudsters.
- There already is a document in place that, when delivered properly with the appraisal, can help protect lenders: the form is the 439 (Appraisers

Representations and Conditions) and should be required to be attached to *every* appraisal.

- When there is a fraudulent appraisal this form will help with a settlement on a claim with insurance companies. Many times the appraiser's insurance carrier modifies this document or the appraiser does not carry insurance. This form should be an underwriting condition, including a copy of the appraiser's license and a statement of the appraiser's errors and omissions insurance, including the carrier's name, contact, policy number and expiration date.
- Providing this information quickly determines the integrity of an appraiser and the insurance coverage could be checked.
- Other steps to take:
  o Set up a special e-mail account for appraisals and have the report e-mailed to processor and underwriting investor at the same time.
  o Get a valid, legible copy of the appraiser's license in every appraisal.
  o Verify the license randomly with the proper licensing agent in each state.

Certifying Verifications & Disclosures:

- All verifications should have an attached disclosure that certifies the mailing or faxing or at least a stamp certifying it is a true copy of the original document.
- Individuals other than the actual verifier—such as processor assistants—should sign the disclosure. It should certify the person that mailed or faxed the verification, when it was mailed and from what location it was mailed.
- This certification will cause a problem for the Mortgage Marauders, as they would now have to enlist a fraudster at the verifier's location.
- If the document is altered the certifier can prove, by retaining their copy, what the original document looked like.
- If the document is altered by retaining their copy the certifier can prove the fraud did not originate with them and would help when resolving a dispute between parties as to whether verification was changed or altered, and by whom.
- Make the individuals stamp all documents or write a certification that they are personally "Certifying this is a true copy of the faxed or original document." Enforcing this will make operational people think twice about what they are given to submit.

Chapter 4:
The 2 Types of Mortgage Fraud

"According to the Federal Bureau of Investigation, bogus checks still account for the majority of the suspicious activity reports filed by federally-related financial institutions. But mortgages have moved up to the second position."

~ Lew Sichelman, from his article *Computer-Savvy Criminals Increasingly Turn to Mortgage Fraud*

As I've said throughout this book, fraud is not just a white-collar crime; it's a *people* crime. People commit it, people suffer in its wake, people's lives are ruined, people enforce it, and it's people like you and I who can prevent it.

Fraud is insidious; it creeps up on you. Fraud exists because it's able to exist. It isn't just the industry that's ripe for manipulation; it's the offices themselves, the paperwork and all its room for error and margins for return. We can't point to any one individual and say, "Look, over there, he's the guy we've been looking for. He's the guy who made it possible for fraud to exist…"

Instead, we must look to ourselves; not as the cause, but the solution. To fight fraud, though, we must first understand it. We must stop seeing fraudsters as criminals and look at them instead for what they really are: colleagues, neighbors, cubicle mates, sometimes even our "friends."

Let's face it: some folks are just plain bad. They're born bad or made bad or just plain *enjoy* being bad. Fraud isn't the only bad thing they do; it's a symptom of a much larger disease that includes everything from lying on their taxes to stiffing waitresses on their tips to pumping gas and driving away because the price of a barrel of oil is too high. I'm not trying to demonize fraudsters, but instead describing what I feel are a minority of those who would commit fraud.

That's right; I said a minority. These types of fraudsters are just taking advantage of an opportunity that already exists. If we could somehow stop all fraud tomorrow I believe that, like cockroaches, these "bad seeds" would quickly find some other way to earn their ill-gotten gains.

I believe the far bigger problem rests in opportunistic fraud. In other words, good people who make bad decisions because an opportunity presents itself, in this case a baroque and antiquated system of forms and procedures that lends itself to mis-reportage and gross negligence.

I believe these are the people we should be targeting, as not only are they less sophisticated than so-called "career criminals" but they're also more likely to be able to be rehabilitated if caught early on. To stem this tide of opportunistic fraudster—and in no way am I condoning their behavior but simply trying to understand and hopefully stop it—let us look to the two main reasons people commit fraud.

Type # 1:
Soft Fraud (to obtain a property)

The first instance of fraud occurs when someone lies about facts to get a loan to buy a property. Although it sounds simple, this can happen on behalf of any or all of the participants involved in obtaining a loan, making it an endemic and widespread issue we all must contend with at some point or another.

From the borrower to the lender and everyone in between—assistants, processors, credit agencies, bike messengers, whoever—fraud to obtain a property is one of the most common ways of duping unsuspecting companies out of their money.

A typical, righteous, and above board scenario for obtaining a property goes something like this: Mr. Future Homeowner sees a property he likes and phones the real estate agent to set up a tour. The property meets his expectations and so he agrees to purchase it. Yay!

At this point, the various wheels that make fraud possible begin to turn, but are ignored by those of us in the industry who want to make an honest living, not a killing. Mr. Homeowner goes to his lender to get a loan. The lender contacts a credit-reporting agency to see if Mr. H is even in the ballpark.

Information is exchanged in order to obtain credit: copy of driver's license, phone number, social security number, the works. Qualified professionals keep this information under wraps and alert the lender that Mr. H does, indeed, qualify for the loan.

Various other agencies get involved—real estate agent, home insurance, title company, etc. After a lot of handshaking, initialing, and signature scrawling, Mr. Homeowner buys his house, above board, and everybody's happy. The real estate agent, credit reporting agency, and title company all get a fee. The lender gets some points on the loan, and as long as Mr. Homeowner keeps paying his mortgage, all goes as planned.

At least, that's how it's *supposed* to happen. When fraud occurs, however, property becomes the vehicle by which illicit gains are obtained. With so many hands in the kettle—the future homeowner, the real estate agent, the loan processor, the credit reporting agency, the lender, and various assistants and collateral employees getting their hands dirty along the way—who's to say where the fraud originates?

In this case the fraudster is usually the would-be property owner. In this scenario, what looks like the most typical homeowner-wannabe is really just an opportunistic predator with knowledge on how to cook the books for one or more of the above agencies to buy their house from shoddy paperwork, which seems above board until they stop the making payments; then suddenly the fraud is uncovered.

This particular fraudster is usually working independently, or with a relative or close friend that's good enough to fool professional lenders like you and I. He learned how to fudge his numbers to the point where they look legitimate; proper verification of down payment money is compromised, or false self-employment income or using false income from a closely held company willing to fudge the real paycheck he or she receives. Thus they get approved for a mortgage to buy their home, and the sad part of this fraud is that with the hundreds of different loan programs available they most likely could have been approved for a loan *without* committing fraud.

Type # 2:
Hard Fraud-to make an immediate profit

The second type of fraud occurs when someone lies about the facts to make an immediate profit. Typically this "someone" is an employee—or several employees—at the lender, real estate company or credit agencies, who are doing so without the knowledge of often unsophisticated or overeager borrowers.

Today's hot real estate market makes everyone an armchair investor, and the promise of quick money from flipped or undervalued properties means plenty of first-time borrowers who are ripe for the picking.

In this scenario, fraudsters in the guise of lenders or credit reporting agencies cook the books so that an avalanche of independently insignificant overcharges line their own pockets while costing the unsuspecting or unsophisticated borrower or lender hundreds or even thousands of dollars in extra, unwarranted fees over the life of the loan. Other times he's in cahoots with a ring of people who can include fellow real estate investors who have influence over one or more of the lending or reporting agencies involved.

This type of fraud is very, very common in the industry, and is just one of the many, many ways in which property is used as the means by which to commit fraud on unsuspecting companies such as yours or mine.

Most times, however, it's a combination of some or all of the above…

Chapter 5:
Hot Fraud Schemes—How to Spot Them; How to Avoid Them

"Fraud and falsehood only dread examination. Truth invites it."

~ Samuel Johnson

There are as many fraud schemes out there today as there are people willing to commit fraud. Every day, it seems, or at least every quarter, the industry responds to a new way to defraud individuals, investors, or companies. These include ALL the various participants of the mortgage loan process, from the consumer to the builder to the realtor to the lender to the borrower.

If nothing else, this list should show you how systemic the problem is, and how many of the key players in our industry are vulnerable to the inherent greed that is part and parcel of committing mortgage fraud.

While it is impossible to list them all here, or even keep up with them all, I have done my best to list those that are still the most prevalent and, indeed, the most likely to come back to haunt you.

In no particular order, here they are:

Rushed Real Estate Closing

This is one of the latest acts of mortgage fraud, and one that lenders are seeing with more and more regularity. In this crime, the fraudsters start a transaction with a very short timeframe in the real estate contract, usually 4–7 days. Next, the real estate agent states to the loan officer "…if the file does not close by the closing date per the contract, the transaction will end."

The loan officer informs the processor that this is in a "super rush mode" and to inform all parties, borrowers, other processors, underwriters, closing departments, appraisers, lender account reps, title closers and others that if this does not close on time "…we will never get a new lead from this real estate agent."

Can you see where fraud might occur in this set-up?

It is important to acknowledge that not all "super rush mortgage files" have a fraudulent intent, but savvy fraudsters have the ability to submit fake documents of all kinds as needed to commit the fraud. The quicker the process, the less likely a savvy loan professional will have the time—or take the time—to check such documents out as properly as they would a longer-term loan limit.

The obvious reason to go along with a "super rush mode file" is that everyone involved is getting paid a commission or bonus so they want to please the real estate agent in order to secure *future* commissions or bonuses. The fraudsters count on this rush as a way for all parties to make errors and/or be pressured to do less than a comprehensive review of all aspects of the transaction to get the "clear to close" on the mortgage, thus the reason for strict pre-funding audit rules.

Owner Occupancy

This may be considered a lesser degree of fraud, but it is still fraud. I honestly don't know why; occupancy misrepresentation, or "fraud for housing," is an extremely serious matter. Borrowers may have every intention to buy, own and pay for their property, but they often falsify their income, residency and other application fields in order to get a specific loan that they would not otherwise qualify for. There are so many loan programs available to these borrowers that they *would* qualify for—maybe loan programs with a little higher interest rate, higher closing costs or both—but at least then they would then not be committing fraud.

Real estate agents and loan officers have experience with this type of fraud, but still the temptation to commit fraud remains a strong one. As always, the choice depends on the individual: sometimes they catch it at the last moment and others let it slide; sometimes they even encourage it, becoming part of the fraud.

If you suspect your borrower is falsifying information, even for a well-founded purpose, you must cancel and stop originating the mortgage. In our industry we should never coach a borrower to lie on their application, or change their information once the application is submitted to you; simply put, it *is* mortgage fraud.

Identity Theft

This is one of the oldest fraudulent acts, most often committed in the past by simply pretending to be someone else for personal gain. Unfortunately, fraudsters are always evolving and while they may not be willing to reinvent the wheel, they sure don't mind spinning it in a brand new direction.

One of the new schemes in this area, for instance, includes the use of a power of attorney given to the fraudster to attend the closing legally, but all the while the power of attorney document is really fake.

In the mortgage industry, this can range from stealing your customer's identity, to borrowers using false names to take out mortgages, to appraisers using another's name to make bad valuations. Victims are usually left with significant monetary losses. When perpetrators are suspected or caught in our industry they are often scuttled away to another unsuspecting mortgage company to be allowed to do it again.

Let's change that, if we can, by preventing mortgage fraud at the outset…

Appraisals

Many lenders state that accurate appraisals are a key point in avoiding mortgage fraud and minimizing the monetary losses. There are two common types of appraisal fraud: stealing an appraiser's identity and wrongful valuations. Whether a property is over- or undervalued, everyone involved in the transaction can be harmed by intentionally creating inaccurate appraisals. But appraisers aren't solely at fault; some fraudsters have learned about electronic "cut and paste" methods to change appraisal information while it is being e-mailed from appraiser to the processor and then it is forwarded on to the underwriter or investor for approval.

One way to slow down this scheme is to have the broker, loan officer or processor instruct the individual appraiser to e-mail the report directly to the underwriting investor. Pressures from mortgage staff and real estate agents to alter borrower's appraisal reports is high, and appraisers express that they don't have an outlet to report inappropriate behavior or requests.

We must never encourage or pressure an appraiser with values, whether in a seemingly positive way, such as with gifts, or in a negative way no matter what their final report states. It is okay to provide an appraiser legitimate supporting documentation to support a value, but not pressure them into higher values if the value does not exist. We need to report to our colleagues and the authorities any fraudulent behavior of appraisals, whether committed by the appraiser or the fraudsters.

Straw Buyers (or Straw Corporations)

In some cases of fraud, homes on the market never actually even have a real buyer but a "straw buyer" instead. In this case, the straw buyer will sign a power of attorney to someone else who happens to have fake credentials, in which they go to the closing and sign the real estate and mortgage closing papers.

Now, remember, on a $200,000 purchase the real estate agent would gross about $5,600, the loan officer would gross about $6,000, in some cases they rented the house for $700–$1,000 per month while not making any mortgage payments, getting away with 7–9 months of collecting rent before the house is foreclosed on. Also, the underwriters and account executives received a bonus and/or commission for the loan. Therefore, it would be my best estimate that each fraudulent transaction grossed our "mortgage marauders" between $15,000 to $20,000 *per transaction*. Now, take a moment to think about the 1 million plus potential fraudulent loan applications in 2005; you do the math!

You should now have no problem using the word "epidemic" any longer…

Property Flipping

Another scenario that's quite common is the quick "land or home flip" deal. This particular type of fraud occurs when an individual or company buys land or a home and sells it immediately for a very inflated price, often 30 to 50 percent higher than the original selling price.

Property flipping is often done in conjunction with appraisal valuation fraud, another reason to work with trusted appraisers. In many cases of property flipping, the fraudster pays a "straw" borrower or non-existent borrower to take out a loan, often with fraudulent appraisals in place.

In this conspiracy, the bad guys buy a starter house or fixer-upper for, say, $200,000. Not an unreasonable price in this inflated real estate market, and certainly not one that's going to raise any eyebrows right off the bat. Happens all the time, right?

No fraud yet. But what happens next is that the bad guys turn around and sells the house to the "straw buyer." Now, some straw buyers know what's happening, others are simply unsophisticated and think they're getting a good deal by being paid a fee to sign some documents. In any event, the "straw buyer" purchases the house for; say $300,000, which he naturally borrows from a lender for the gain of the bad guys.

The bad guys profit and the "straw buyer" defaults on the loan, most of the time never making the first payment, leaving behind a lender who's just been defrauded of $100,000—and more, if you count the hard and soft costs related to the transaction.

To combat this type of fraud, the wholesale investors need the retail originating team to perform our industry best practices. They will thank you for your originating due diligence, along with wholesale investor's due diligence in underwriting. The originators and the wholesale investors need a careful review of the title policy, watching the chain of ownership, checking the borrower's home background, requesting recent MLS sales in that area, and getting a second appraisal if the value or loan numbers do not make sense.

Social Security Number Identity Theft or Fraud

We have talked at length about what a vital piece of information a client's social security card is—and just how secure that information should remain—but despite all of that, or perhaps because of that, social security number identity theft or fraud remains high on the list of fraudster favorites.

Here are certain red flags to be on the lookout for in order to avoid this devastating theft of identity:

- **Is it a valid number?** Run verification checks available with on-line services (see our fraud resource section at the back of this book or on my website for more information).
- **Does it match in all areas of the file?**
- **Is the issued number consistent with the age of the borrower?**
- **Where do bad SS# numbers come from:**
    o *Transposed Numbers*
    o *Use of a Deceased Person's number*
    o *Use of a child's or a minor's SSN*
    o *Use of a Tax ID number*

Although it seems anathema to those of us who are in this industry for the right reasons, you would be surprised by how common this theft is, and how weak the penalties for it are. As an example of both, here are just two of the dozens of cases I read for this book and how they ended up:

Sooner or later they get caught!

When police in Cleveland, Tenn., pulled over a car, they thought they had nabbed some small time drug dealers and would be counterfeiters. Instead police bagged a couple of New York fugitives who have been linked to a $2 million mortgage fraud case in Buffalo and who have been on the run since 2002. The two of them were wanted on charges that they were involved in a scheme to defraud lenders out of loans. They bought about 40 dilapidated properties for a total cost of about $120,000, but then used fraud to get second mortgages that totaled about $2 million.

Sooner or later they get caught!
(Again!)

An alert real estate company helped Maryland police catch a woman accused of stealing an identity to get a $400,000 mortgage loan. The real estate company said it found discrepancies that gave hints that the she wasn't who she said she was. The company contacted the woman whose name was used in applying for the loan. And sure enough, the victim said she had not applied for a mortgage and frankly "…did not know what the real estate company was talking about." A mortgage company in Missouri said it had approved a loan in the victim's name. When the identity thief met with a real estate agent at the house, police showed up and arrested her…

Fake Employers

These last two items have cropped up with increasing frequency and are so new they may not be common knowledge. (At least, they weren't to me.) This first tactic, in particular, is so ingenious that it blew my mind at first, and I suppose that is the ploy on which fraudsters rely: those of us who would never think of committing fraud find it hard to believe some of the tactics the bad guys come up with! In this case, two fraudulent parties are involved.

The first is a company who offers services to various "clients." The client then completes an application to become an independent contractor for the parent company; we'll call them XYZ Company. XYZ Company claims the client as an "employee" so that they can have a verifiable employee on their various loan documents, and in exchange the "employee" pays XYZ Company a percentage of the desired "annual income" in exchange for Verifications of Employment.

So, let's say the fake employee needs to put down a fake annual income of 50,000 fake dollars a year. For the privilege, they must pay their fake "employer" $500. In this scenario, both bad guys clean up: XYZ Company does nothing but provide a shell employer for their clients, and rakes in hundreds to thousands of dollars for each client. The fake employee only needs to pay a few hundred to a few thousand dollars for the privilege of making thousands to tens of thousands in fraudulent income. Not bad for a day's work!

Fake Organizations
(For Anything They Are Missing)

This crime is promoted as a way to help "save" clients that might be lost due to the client's inability to show sufficient assets. As we all know, this is a common problem in our industry and one that causes much frustration for those of us who are close to a deal. Still, I contend that it's better to lose a deal for legitimate reasons than make a deal based on a lie.

Who do you think the FBI agrees with?

Here's how it works: XYZ Company establishes an account in the client's name and places money and/or assets into the account. This money or these assets are in turn "rented" from XYZ Company for a fee of 5% of the value of whatever funds have been deposited. For the next month, which as we all know is the typical amount it takes for a loan to process, this bogus XYZ Company will produce written or verbal asset verifications to creditors, vendors, and lenders.

Chapter 6:
Understanding the Whole Transaction—The Usual Suspects (and How to Spot Them)

"Any informed borrower is simply less vulnerable to fraud and abuse."
~ Alan Greenspan

Mortgage fraud is like a one-act play—one whose effects last long after the curtain closes and the audience goes home. Like a play, actors in the drama play their part to perfection. Some of us are the good guys; others are the bad guys. Some of us play leading parts, others are merely extras, watching from the sidelines and not exactly malicious but certainly culpable.

Which role will you play? Well, of course, that's entirely up to you. Every play needs a director and that's where you come in. But how will you know who is playing what and how big a role they'll play? With so many hands in the pot, it's easy to see how mortgage fraud can be as alluring as it is profitable.

I've never been to a play where they didn't give me a Playbill so I could follow the characters and know who they are. Well, that's what I'm giving you here. In this chapter you will meet all the players in the game, from the consumer to the lender, and everyone in between.

Along the way we'll meet the real estate agents, the title reps, even the builders. Yes, the most obvious players as well as the least obvious play their part well, and the only way to foil the mystery and emerge as the good guys in the end is to recognize them before they lure us into their web of deceit.

I start with something that's developed recently but that will be of use to us all in the long run, The Patriot Act. It's fairly complicated, so let's waste no time in examining this compelling new development:

The Patriot Act
Section 326 of the USA PATRIOT Act Requires a Customer Identification Program

Effective October 1, 2005, your originators must submit the following information on all applicants and co-applicants before you should process any credit applications:

1. Customer's Full Name.
2. Customer's Physical Street Address.
3. Customer's Date of Birth.
4. Customer's Social Security Number.

You need to inform your originators, and they should acknowledge that they are required to provide notification to all applicants to comply with the provisions of the USA PATRIOT Act and to provide the identifying information as requested to complete the processing of all loan applications.

Per the Customer Identification Program, the following notice MUST be given to all Applicants:

IMPORTANT INFORMATION ABOUT PROCEDURES:

To help the government fight the funding of terrorism and money laundering activities, Federal law requires all financial institutions to obtain, verify, and record information that identifies each person who opens an account.

What this means for you:

When you apply for a new loan, we will ask for your name, address, date of birth, and other information that will allow us to identify you. We may also ask to see your driver's license or other identifying documents.

The Patriot act was written with the intent to battle terrorism, yet surprisingly it has several provisions that should be helping in the battle against mortgage fraud. In fact, one part from section 314-b of the law should benefit mortgage fraud prevention quite specifically as it provides what is known as "information-sharing" among parties involved or involving a financial transaction, which should bring the real estate transaction into the act if it contains fraud.

I'm sure you can see the benefits of sharing information. We all need to create, utilize and implement a plan to "know who you are doing business with," which definitely includes identifying clients properly within the guidelines of the loan being requested.

This is the area of your business where new and professional employee training and pre-funding audits come into play. We need to put verifiable systems in place to keep measurements and to identify mortgage loan files that should not be funded, thus stopping mortgage fraud one file at a time.

I am not an attorney, but simply reviewing this act reveals that if the lenders and their attorneys were to really take a hard look at the Patriot Act, they should be able to find ways that would make it easy to comply and to know who they are funding a loan for.

Who is originating the loan or fraud scheme to share with other lenders without fear, which again establishes the need for strong pre-funding quality control procedures? This would help to track individual fraudsters in each market. When talking about this some management will balk at the additional time or expense to implement such a plan, but these are usually the members of upper management that have not yet been directly victimized by fraud! So we all need to remember three things that offset the initial cost of such endeavors.

They are:

1. **The civil penalties for non-compliance;**
2. **The criminal penalties for non-compliance;**
3. **The internal and external cost of a fraudulent mortgage...**

Just hearing the words "civil or criminal penalties for not complying with proper standards and procedures" should make you cringe, but in case they don't, let's take these serious penalties one at a time:

Patriot Act Penalties

Patriot Act penalties themselves are stiff, as they could include companies and their officers and are subject to civil and criminal penalties. When it comes to willful criminal acts, they can be fined up to $500,000 per day depending on how they violate the act.

On the civil part of the act the fine could be as much as $25,000 per day. (Ouch!) The reason the Patriot Act can be so beneficial to our industry in particular is because of the way we use information, and how easily that information can be altered using today's technology in the hands of motivated fraudsters.

For instance, in my investigations of the Primero scheme I was told that in several places in the Denver metro area, or for that matter any city, for only $150.00 to $1,000.00 a person could get some very good identification for the means of defrauding any one of the individuals involved in the mortgage loan process.

Of course, the price depends on how many sources you are requesting. What sources of information, you ask? Well, they include driver's license, social security card, green cards, paycheck stubs, W-2 forms and verification of this information, if needed. (Did I just hear you say "WOW?" because that it is what I said upon learning this information!) The question I have is what do most mortgage companies do with this information when they discover the fraudulent documents?

Based on the Patriot Act law it seems very clear what we *should* be doing, but because we as an industry do not share this information, the borrower and the fraudsters simply keep submitting the loan until they find a wholesale investor that will give them the "clear to close."

External Losses of a Fraudulent Mortgage

External losses are directly related to the actual money lost associated with a fraudulent loan. Now, most of the larger mortgage lenders have a specific strategy in place with an action plan once the fraud is uncovered, but all of us should realize what the actual costs can include, i.e. shortage on outstanding principal balance, accrued interest, real estate fees to resell the property, legal costs and any repairs to the home needed in order to have it ready to sell again.

After determining how much the losses are each mortgage lender must decide what the proper course of action is. For instance, do they pursue civil litigation or criminal prosecution—or even both? To consider civil action there has to be a dollar amount they have in mind as a threshold to determine if it is worth the action. (Anyone who's ever had to hire a lawyer knows the inherent costs in pursuing such a drastic course of action.)

If it is a criminal action we should have no doubt what we should do: Report the fraud! The issue that I uncovered at Primero was that all of the mortgage loans had 100% financing utilizing the seller assisted down payment gift program inherent in an FHA loan.

What does this mean, exactly? Well, a couple of things. For starters, if the borrower knew he/she committed fraud and is called out for it, what do they care about the house? After all, they will only live in it for 6–9 months for free or move out and rent the house, but not make payments. If the home is bought by someone with fraudulent identification who is in this country illegally, he or she will most likely just move out, get some new I.D.'s and leave the house vacant.

These are just two of the dozens of scenarios I could relate here, based on my own experience alone.

The basic premise is that these fraudsters know they have either made money for profit or they have zero money invested in the home so they do not have the emotional attachment that honest, hard working people have to their homes. The homeowners I contacted that did not realize that the fraudsters committed fraud in getting their home loan approved worked very hard with Primero to correct the issues in order to own their home legally.

Internal Losses of a Fraudulent Mortgage

Internal losses. Now, this is an area that most lenders have trouble dealing with when it comes to fraud, but they need to understand that while they can eventually calculate the exact external losses it's very difficult to accurately calculate the internal loss when fraud occurs.

For instance, rehiring staff and the intensive training that goes with that process (and do we train the same way all over again), can get very costly but it's the only way to make sure that not only are you doing your due diligence in preventing fraud through new hiring but you're working hard to prevent it in your own backyard.

You can also lose market share in a couple of areas, your reputation with the local community and reputation with warehouse lenders, your wholesale investors, with institutions like HUD, or even the termination of some very important lending agreements. (And aren't they all, really?) It is easy to see that the internal losses can be much larger than the actual costs and money lost on the loan itself.

The bottom line here is that it should seem very obvious and clear that the cost to implement a clear pre-funding quality control audit plan on one loan at a time far outweighs the cost of what can happen when mortgage fraud is discovered in post-closing instead.

The Consumer
(Or Buyer)

Beware when a loan application looks too good to be true. As I've said over and over throughout this book, that usually means it IS too good to be true. Yet today's savvy consumers who would commit fraud know that their best way to a smooth loan process is to avoid as many red flags as possible.

Since most of us look for trouble rather than trouble-free as a sign of fraud, such fraudsters on the consumer end know to make their loan applications look as good as they can. They do this in various ways, and thanks to modern technology often get away with creating documents that look as good, if not better, than the real thing.

Buyers can stand alone in the fraud dilemma, or they can work in cahoots with one or more links in the mortgage process chain. Either way, a buyer who initiates or even cooperates in a fraudulent loan is culpable for more than just duping a lender.

They are, quite literally, committing a crime...

The Real Estate Agent

One of the most overlooked players in the fraud game is the real estate agent (remember as I talk about this that I am a licensed real estate agent).

In fact, recent articles in the press indicate that some of those involved in real estate settlements may not fully understand their obligations under the RESPA, or Real Estate Settlement Procedures Act.

The common denominator in almost all home sales—the real estate agent involved in real estate fraud—should not get such a free pass from those of us in the rest of the industry. Yet in spite of their pivotal role in the birth of the mortgage loan process, many agents seem to have an attitude that they are not involved in the mortgage so they can give advice to buyers or lenders—or even commit outright fraud—and it will not affect them; only the lender.

Part of this growing trend may be mere negligence; another part may simply be getting away with it while they can. After all, with all of the emphasis put on the loan processors, consumers, and lenders, it may seem like the time has never been better for real estate agent initiated fraud.

There are many opportunities for a savvy real estate agent to get involved in fraud, either knowingly or innocently. In essence they are the middlemen between all of these various agencies; the spoke in the money wheel, if you will.

They are in touch with the buyers, the lenders, the title company, the insurance reps, the builders, the contractors; you name it, a good real estate agent will have his finger right in the middle of it.

Add to this already alarming potential for wrongdoing the fact that real estate agents require little if any formal ethics training. An expensive class, a state test, a shingle to hang out, and your typical real estate agent can be in business in less than a few months. Certainly, I'm not trying to disparage an entire industry because of a few—though, of course, it is more than a few—bad apples, but clearly the opportunity for fraud exists when you have a steady influx of new, inexperienced, and often unsophisticated real estate agents.

For instance, what happens when the market goes soft and the agent who was making tens of thousands of dollars in commissions a month with little to no effort suddenly has to scramble and work overtime to make only a fraction of that? By fudging a few handy figures on a few loan apps, the same agent can be back in the money in no time. Are we to believe that no real estate agents have surmised the exact same scenario?

To avoid having agents knowingly or unwittingly commit fraud, they should have much more training on the "Do's and Don'ts" for real estate brokers and associates.

The Builder

So far we've concentrated on discussions centering on the white-collar criminals involved in the process of fraud. The office workers, clerks, and other professionals that handle the money end of the mortgage loan.

But like real estate agents, builders also have their finger on the pulse of the mortgage process. Builders know contractors; builders know appraisers. Builders know real estate agents; builders know customers.

If the real estate agent is like the spoke in the middle of the money wheel, then the builder is like the pedal. They alone create the product, around which some of this fraud is whirling, for without new buildings to buy no home mortgages would exist. Knowing this, why do we assume they are above suspicion when it comes to fraudulent activity?

The short answer is, "they're not." The longer answer involves placing stricter guidelines on all parts of the so-called "money wheel," including the real estate agent and the builders, two key players who until now we've not yet fully discussed. I am not saying that all builders are committing fraud; we have some very honest hard working home builders in this country.

Industry guidelines should exist across the board, from white collar to blue collar criminals. Checks and balances shouldn't include everybody *except* the realtors or the builders; they should be all-inclusive. Only by policing every part of the mortgage chain will we find the weakest link.

Or, as is usually the case, the weakest *links*...

The Title Company

Speaking from experience, the title company plays a massive part in the loan process. After all, they determine insurability and track the title changes or information for the purposes of the loan. Perhaps that's why many such companies are the first to be caught up in the numerous instances of fraud that occur every day. Here is just a brief rundown of the latest:

- The title company agreed to a $680,000 settlement after HUD claimed that the company, doing business as Memphis Title, made payments through sham affiliated businesses in the Memphis area in violation of RESPA's anti-kickback and unearned fee provisions.
- The Michigan-based title company has agreed to fork over $150,000 on charges that it violated RESPA's office rental regulations by paying brokers kickbacks disguised as conference room rental fees—fees which HUD alleged were based on rates that were "substantially higher" than their fair market value.
- A settlement reached with a title company calls for the company to cease its use of inducements given or paid to real estate agents in exchange for the referral of business. The title company's response to the settlement is that the company has always strived to operate with integrity, and that California has not clearly defined its own laws.

Obviously, we could go on and on but as a frequent follower of such cases I can tell you from experience that, after awhile, they all start to sound alike. The players may change, the towns and cities and states and companies, but the accusations and fraud remains the same.

Don't take my word for it. Many an expert has weighed in on the subject, including Phil Schulman, partner with the Washington D.C. firm Kirkpatrick & Lockhart Nicholson Graham LLP, who when speaking at the National Settlement Services Summit being held in Cleveland recently had this to say about the matter:

> *"Getting money into the hands of real estate brokers and builders, of course, is what title agents live for. And so, I'm going to help you to make your day. There are things you can do to pay people upstream without violating RESPA."*

The Mortgage Lender
(Understanding the Process)

The mortgage lending industry originates, sells, and services mortgages secured by residential, multifamily and commercial real estate. As one might imagine, and most of us know from experience, the mortgage lending process is a complex series of interrelated activities, which offers you a number of different job opportunities. To help you understand the key players involved in committing mortgage fraud, let's first review the various activities associated with mortgage lending.

The Mortgage Broker
(The retail mortgage company)

Origination is the creation of mortgage applications. Loan originators (loan officers and brokers) are the sales force in the real estate finance industry. "Loan officers" work directly for a lending institution. "Brokers" are agents for various lending institutions, matching the borrower with the most appropriate loan program. Whether a loan officer or a broker, the loan originator initiates the origination process by locating borrowers and making loan applications.

Processing

Processing is the collection of documentation and verifications to support information provided on the loan application. Among the documents obtained by the processor are the appraisal, which confirms the value of the mortgaged property, a credit report, which discloses the borrower's credit history, employment history and housing history and more if required by the wholesale investor.

Underwriting

Underwriting is the evaluation of loan documentation to approve or deny the loan. During the evaluation process, the underwriter analyzes whether the loan represents an acceptable risk to the lender. The underwriter is the final verifier in the loan, an important aspect of the evaluation process in determining whether the loan meets the requirements that make it saleable to investors in the secondary mortgage market.

Closing

Closing is the consummation of the loan transaction. The closing process involves the final loan amount and closing costs, delivery of a deed, the signing of the closing package including the mortgage note, and the disbursement of loan funds.

Warehousing

Warehousing is the method by which most mortgage bankers fund the loans at closing. Warehousing involves short-term borrowing of funds from warehouse banks using permanent mortgage loans as collateral. The money borrowed from this line of credit is used to produce mortgage loans. Once the loans are sold to an investor on the secondary market, the mortgage banker replenishes the warehouse line, enabling it to use the funds to create more loans.

Shipping and Delivery

Shipping and delivery is the packaging of closed loan files for delivery to an investor. This consummates the loan sale and all activities associated with "loan production."

Secondary Marketing

Secondary marketing is the sale of closed loans to investors, the development and pricing of loan programs, and the management of the risk associated with funding mortgages. Normally, the sale to investors is arranged simultaneously with the origination of loans. Commitments are used to secure the future sale of loans and protect against interest rate changes that may occur between the dates of origination and sale.

Loan Servicing and Administration

Loan servicing and administration is the collection, recording and remittance of monthly mortgage payments to investors. Servicing also includes the maintenance of escrows; the majority of the time the servicing mortgage company is paying for the borrower their hazard insurance and property taxes to protect the property that secures each loan.

Chapter 7:
The Lure (Don't Buy In)—Some Loan Fraud May Seem Minor, but Fraud is Fraud!

"A borrower has the right to clear and forthright explanations of the terms and conditions of a loan…"

~ From "The Borrower's Bill of Rights,"
www.stopmortgagefraud.com

First and foremost, know this: Fraud is a crime. Second, ignorance does not equal innocence. As an industry, as professionals, as colleagues, as supervisors, as employees, as individuals it is up to us to fight fraud collectively and singularly; otherwise, we're just as culpable as the fraudsters themselves.

Before we continue our discussion of the "The Lure," let's be clear on this one thing: loan fraud occurs when a lender makes an inappropriate loan, because the property is overvalued or the lender has a false picture of the buyer's financial position.

It's often done with the best of intentions, but manipulating contracts, appraisals, sources of down payment, and sale prices to help buyers qualify for a higher loan amount—even if it's suggested by the borrower, real estate professional or the lender—*is* fraud. The problem is that, unlike you, most of our colleagues are simply not proactive about identifying, preventing, or reporting fraud.

Now, I'm not saying I was any different from anyone else in this industry. In fact, before fraud happened to me I was just as uninformed as the rest. I was busy, I worked hard, I subscribed to the industry periodicals, I read the *Wall Street Journal*, I vetted my employees carefully, and I supervised them well. What more could I do?

Well, I'm here to tell you that you're never too busy to become a victim of fraud. That should be sobering news. You can work as hard as the next guy—harder, even—but I can guarantee you that a motivated fraudster is working twice as hard to dupe you into being defrauded.

No matter how hard you work, you will never, ever be able to control the will of another human being. Fraudsters can work with you, bowl with you, eat dinner with you, come to your house for holidays, come early, stay late, and score 30 points every weekend in the league basketball games, but if they want to commit fraud—and you're willing to let them either through ignorance or bliss—they *will* find a way.

So the choice is clear: Be vigilant against fraud and avoid it or look the other way and become a victim. What's it gonna be? For me, the choice was clear. To reassure you, I will say that now that I've put the various safeguarding procedures in place in my own company, I don't work any harder than I ever did. Fraud may be insidious, but so is its cure. Little by little, day-by-day, I find myself learning more and fighting harder to prevent fraud.

Is it harder? Sure. I wish fraud didn't exist but, as we now know, it does. Is it difficult? Not really. Not once you learn the ins and outs that I'm teaching you here, and on my website at www.preventmortgagefraud.com.

Is it impossible?

No way…

If I can do it, *you* can do it. It's just that simple. Now, there are many steps to avoid fraud but the first and foremost is to resist it yourself. The lure of easy money is a powerful one, and those of us who manage to avoid it all our lives can often fall prey without even realizing it, if we're not careful.

Fraudsters stalk their prey no differently than do lions in the jungle. They can spot weakness from across a crowded office and pick up cues better than a frat boy on the prowl down Sorority Row. They are cunning, smart, and shrewd, and the lures they use revolve around the oldest of all pursuits: money.

It's easy in these busy times in this industry to let things go by that might not normally be overlooked. Fraudsters prey on you whether it's busy or slow. Here's how: Let's say you run a small mortgage company with a dozen employees. You run a tight ship, or so you think, and your top loan originator has been with you for three or four years. You know her, she knows you, and both you and your employees trust her. Business is good, nobody's looking, and one day she submits a loan application to underwriting that needs just a little "tweaking" to pass muster. Nothing much, just an inflated appraisal value is needed from the appraiser here or modified verification there.

It's one out of maybe twenty your company submitted for approval that week. Who's going to notice, right? This is the lure, this is the come-on, and this is the dupe. This is how good people go bad; a little at a time. First it's this form, next week it's another, and before you know it there's one a week, then one a day.

A quick buck here, a few grand there, and soon she and your company are committing fraud, the company in most cases is unknowingly participating. It's blunt, but it's true. Changing information yourself, or even letting someone knowingly change information; is fraud. If you're doing it; it's fraud. If you're letting someone do it; it's fraud. If you even suspect someone's doing it; it's fraud.

You must resist.

You must identify.

You must prevent.

You must report.

It's just that simple…

Prevention (With Protection)

Of course, all of this collection of information is designed simply to start building a case against whoever committed the fraud, be it the broker, the loan officer, the verifier, or the employer. When you *do* find fraud here are a few steps to perform for your own individual protection:

- Have a written explanation of how you discovered the alleged fraud;
- Document what the consequences of the fraud involved;
- Make notes of anyone involved in the mortgage transaction;
- Document what part of the transaction is involving fraud;
- Record details about your suspicions, and proof on how you found out about the fraud;
- Report the misrepresentation;
- Inform your company's fraud expert, legal department and/or manager;
- Do not get discouraged if you do not see immediate results;
- Do not withhold any information, even if you believe it to be insignificant;
- Do not lie, mislead, or otherwise provide false information;
- Do not delay any requests for additional info or documents from authorities…

A Word on Ethnicity in Fraud

As we wind up our discussion of the extremely powerful mortgage fraud lure—and how powerful it really is—I thought it might be appropriate to mention here that fraud does not discriminate. The majority of us are as susceptible as the minority, and vice versa.

There is mortgage fraud in every market, whether it's reported or not, while the different schemes and fraudsters seem to be ethnic based; depending on ethnicity there seems to be different patterns of fraud.

This is not to say it is discrimination, but mortgage fraud today has a pattern within each individual scheme seeming to target a specific ethnic group. The trust level within each of these ethnic groups is higher, whether for committing fraud or protecting the fraudsters. It is not to be said that people of different race or ethnic groups will not work together committing fraud.

Chapter 8:
Do Not Become a Victim—What to Look Out For

"It is a fraud to borrow what we are unable to pay."
~ Publilius Syrus

Mortgage fraud prevention should be a daily part of your experience in the mortgage lending industry. I have tried to make it a constant theme in this book. Some of this material may be a refresher course for you but as I have learned, it is never too early—or too common—to hear how to prevent yourself from falling victim to mortgage fraud. To that end, here is a quick reminder of the Top-3 ways to protect yourself:

- **Have checks and balances in place to know your brokers or loan officers and their preferred relationships:** With most mortgage fraud it is best—and easiest—to avoid when you catch it early, prior to funding the loan. By having a strong system of checks and balances—a safety net, if you will—you will not only know when fraud is occurring but who is originating it. If you do nothing else please, *please* don't overlook this basic step in preventing fraud. After all, the fraudsters know that the industry is currently disorganized and behind on finding and stopping fraud. The goal is to catch fraud before a loan closes, and treat attempted fraud with the same severity as a closed, fraudulent loan. Checks and balances are the best way to ensure that first, crucial step is taken, and taken quickly!

- **Establish or strengthen pre-funding controls and understand how the bad guys do business:** This book is only the beginning. By being made aware of the mentality and madness of fraudsters all over the country, it is my hope that you are now not just cognizant of the epidemic, nor that you feel that word is still too strong, but that you are proactive about moving forward in your own personal campaign of fraud prevention. No such campaign would be complete without a basic understanding of how fraudsters operate. I believe I've done just that; given you the "basics," but there is much, much more to learn. I'm still learning something new every day, and no book could ever encompass all of the various methodologies, scams, and warning signs that exist to identify, prevent, and report fraud. We must be vigilant, but we must be self-starters. Use this book as a tool, not as a Bible, and begin an active campaign that starts with YOU!

- **Hire professional examiners for pre-funding and post-funding training and audits:** When fraud happened to me, I looked inward first and then outward. The advances I've been able to make in identifying, preventing, and reporting fraud could not have been made alone.

Of course, these reminders are just the beginning, and we will discuss several more as we wend our way through this challenging, perilous, and all-important journey through fraud prevention.

Obviously, knowledge is our strongest ally in the war on these daring fraudsters. Perhaps right now I'm sharing that knowledge with you, but the two of us can only do so much. As I will continue to teach others it is imperative that you do the same, starting in your own company, office, or even cubicle.

When educating real estate agents, borrowers, processors, underwriters, appraisers, lender account reps, and title closers to take action against mortgage fraud, there are a few steps to perform for your own individual protection.

For instance, you need to have a written explanation detailing how you discovered the alleged fraud and report the misrepresentation and what the consequences of the fraud involves, make notes of anyone involved in the mortgage or the part of the transaction involving fraud, give details about your suspicions, proof of how you found out about the fraud (and is it verified) and then inform your company's fraud expert contact, legal department and manager to whom you report to.

Do not get discouraged if you do not see immediate results, do not withhold information, and even if you believe it to be insignificant do not lie, mislead, or otherwise provide false information and be sure not to delay any requests for additional information or documents from authorities.

Code of Ethics for Real Estate Professionals:

Although it seems strange that we have a list of such common sense traits to look for in real estate professionals, the prevalence of fraud in our industry makes it such that I feel the need to include the following Code of Ethics for Real Estate Professionals (and if you're wondering, this comes from my own company):

- **Honesty and integrity...** we conduct business in a manner reflecting honesty, honor, and integrity.
- **Professional conduct...** we conduct business activities in a professional manner.
- **Honesty in advertising...** we endeavor to be accurate in all advertising and solicitations.
- **Confidentiality...** we avoid unauthorized disclosure of confidential information.
- **Compliance with the law...** we conduct business in compliance with all applicable laws and regulations.
- **Disclosure of financial interest...** we disclose any equity or financial interest we may have in the collateral being offered to secure a loan.

Two Types of Due Process
(And Why They're Long Overdue)

As we've seen throughout this book, prevention and detection are only two parts of the process. Apprehension and punishment should be equally important in stopping fraud once and for all. The following are the two different types of legal processes—and how they work:

Federal Criminal Prosecution Process

- Allegation
- Investigation
- Grand Jury
- Indictment/information
- Discovery
- Trial
- Sentencing

Civil Prosecution Process

- ➤ Usually the standard of evidence is less than what is needed for criminal prosecution…
  - Allegation
  - Investigation
  - Plaintiff files complaint
  - Discovery/disposition
  - Litigants are encouraged to resolve the issue before trial with a settlement of some type
  - Trial
  - Damages are paid to the plaintiff if found guilty

How Lenders Can Be Protected

All right, enough of the bad news. Knowledge is key in this process, but action is prevention and right now we're going to learn various avenues we can explore to begin protecting ourselves right now, today.

In the face of so much doom and gloom—the sobering statistics, the disappointment in people, and the many opportunities for fraud—it is hard not to feel powerless in the face of the bad guys and what they seem to accomplish so easily—and so often.

But while we can't control their actions, we can control our own…

Prevention is the number one resources afforded us. We can learn, grow, adapt, challenge ourselves, and mystify those who would commit fraud by fighting fire with fire. Only if we begin taking fraud as seriously as the fraudsters will we ever hope to defeat them. To that end I am outlining here the first steps toward preventing appraisal fraud—and protecting ourselves.

To prevent appraisal fraud we must maintain internal databases:

- To verify history;
- To check for better comparables;
- To check for prior association with property address and/or application;
- To update training for underwriters and reviewers…

To prevent fraud we must take advantage of technology:

- To review appraisals;
- To track and monitor individuals involved in the loan;
- To increase quality and efficiency while reducing time;
- To update checklists and instructions to appraisers…

To prevent fraud we must monitor appraiser quality:

- Issue direct guidelines;
- Require compliance from appraisers;
- Keep tracking record on appraisers and hold appraisers accountable;
- Shift focus from fixing errors…to preventing them.

We will get more specific about the other loan fraud prevention techniques in later chapters, but for now I thought we could all use a shot in the arm. Hopefully now we can feel more empowered to continue on this journey and discover even more ways to protect ourselves—and prosecute the bad guys.

By this point you might be asking yourself, "Why should I go to all this trouble? Nobody's going to help me in this world, why should I help in the fight against fraudsters? What's anyone in my industry done for ME lately?"

True; these are all valid questions. I recognize that seeing the small picture is sometimes easier than seeing the big one. Our industry is so big, so anonymous, so hard to imagine in all its entirety, often it's natural to feel lost in the shuffle and to imagine ourselves the lone gunslinger ambling down Main Street all by our lonesome to face a passel of evildoers.

Well, fine; let's bring it down to the personal level for you. I'll lay it out as simply as possible: failure to report, or even trying to prevent, fraud can mean that not only are you a victim of all the havoc those fraudsters wreak in your company, but you could be held both civilly and, what's worse, CRIMINALLY, as an accomplice.

That's right: an accomplice. It's called "willful blindness" and it's a new concept worth exploring a little more fully before we move on to the next chapter, which involves the two main reasons people commit fraud.

Willful Blindness

The world isn't fair, and nowhere is that truth more evident than when discussing the concept of willful blindness, which at its heart expresses the contention that the industry exhibited "willful blindness" to obvious fraud through ignoring it for so long, in so many cases, at the hands of so many fraudsters.

To be honest, fraud does not exist in a vacuum. It arises from opportunity, and more often than not that opportunity exists because we are too busy minding the high-rise to success that we're working so hard to build to check on the rats steadily chewing away at our foundations.

Willful blindness is a legal term that skirts the boundary between neglect and culpability, and I wouldn't be able to talk about it if it didn't exist. It's here, it's here to stay, and if we don't look out we could be accused of it through no fault of our own. At its heart the letter of law assumes that we create the "intent" necessary in establishing criminal liability. One court's definition reads thusly:

> *"One who, knowing or strongly suspecting that he is involved in shady dealings and who takes steps to make sure that he does not acquire full or exact knowledge of the nature of those dealing is held to have criminal intent."*

While common in criminal cases, especially related to money laundering and software infringement cases, "willful blindness" is also being used increasingly to ascribe civil liability to companies in the financial services industry.

Please don't think I'm trying to scare you. As we saw with my story, the investigative process into any type of fraud is very long and very involved, and you would have ample opportunity to plead your case and innocence.

However, in those instances when it comes down to their word against yours, who will the court believe? Chances are it would be you, but do you really want to leave that up to chance simply because you didn't pay attention to the red flags that invariably pop up when fraud rears its ugly head?

I didn't think so…

> **REMEMBER:**
>
> *The more aggressive a lender is in working with brokers to make deals work, the more aggressive that lender must be in discovering, preventing and reporting fraud.*

For detailed information about these documents, lists, action steps, preventative measures, and procedures, as well as various other handy resources, please: visit my website at www.preventmortgagefraud.com—or see some of the templates I've included at the back of this book.

I have found that since I've created these documents the atmosphere at my company is one of forthrightness and willingness to share. Today it is an open office, where secrets can no longer hide. As such, they've helped me immeasurably and it is my hope that they might help you as well.

Please give them a look and help your company fight fraud right now, today. Although it is always good to have these documents in writing it is very important to review and go over the details verbally with each person to assure they understand the purpose of a company having these kinds of documents in place.

In the meantime, I have included for your convenience the following Fraud Prevention and Quality Control Self-test, which will help you identify the various red flags and warning signs in your own organization, as well as most of the duties being required by HUD for you to perform.

Fraud Prevention & Quality Control Self-test

Yes—No Please check appropriate box

Your Pre-Funding Q.C. Plan Questions

- ➤ ___ ___ You verify borrower's employment prior to funding your loan.
- ➤ ___ ___ You ensure you have the proper chain of title.
- ➤ ___ ___ You do a credit liability review of credit reports in the submitted file.
- ➤ ___ ___ You do data integrity checks of documents provided, VOE, VOD, VOR.
- ➤ ___ ___ You verify social security numbers.
- ➤ ___ ___ You do occupancy checks or verifications.
- ➤ ___ ___ You ensure property value with previous sale/market value research.
- ➤ ___ ___ You verify ownership records, if self-employed, are valid.

Your Post-Funding Q.C. Plan Questions

- ➤ ___ ___ The mortgage maintains compliance with HUD/FHA requirements.
- ➤ ___ ___ The personnel conducting the QC reviews have no direct loan processing, origination, or underwriting responsibilities.
- ➤ ___ ___ You have periodic reports that identify deficiencies and are provided to senior management within one month of completion of the initial report.
- ➤ ___ ___ The personnel are properly trained and have access to HUD/FHA guidelines; procedures are revised to reflect changes in FHA requirements and personnel are informed of the changes.

➤ ___ ___ You have prompt, effective corrective measures that are taken by senior management and documented when deficiencies are identified.

➤ ___ ___ You have procedures in place for expanding the scope of the QC review when fraud or patterns of deficiencies are uncovered.

➤ ___ ___ You, the mortgagee, or a QC company reviews EITHER:
- 10% of all loans closed on a monthly basis; OR
- A random sample that provides 95% confidence level with 2% precision.

➤ ___ ___The selection includes loans from all branches.

➤ ___ ___The selection includes loans from all authorized agents, loan correspondents.

➤ ___ ___The selection includes loans from all loan officers, underwriters, and loan processors.

➤ ___ ___The selection includes loans from all FHA programs.

➤ ___ ___The selection includes loans from appraisers, real estate companies, and builders with whom you do a significant amount of business.

➤ ___ ___Each Q.C. has a system to review documents giving an example of how the sample size and selections were determined

➤ ___ ___ Loans that go into default within the first 6 months are reviewed.

➤ ___ ___ Sponsors of loan correspondents perform QC reviews on loans purchased from their correspondents.

➤ ___ ___An on-site branch office review is completed.

➤ ___ ___A review of alternative document loans is completed.

➤ ___ ___You are reporting to HUD or appropriate Fed. Agency under HMDA.

➤ ___ ___The mortgagee reports any violation of law or regulation, false statement of program abuse to HUD HOC or OIG within 60 days of discovery.

➤ ___ ___The personnel at all offices are employees of the mortgage company or contract employees performing functions that HUD allows to be outsourced.

➤ ___ ___MIP's are remitted within 15 days from closing.

➤ ___ ___No one is employed who is debarred, suspended or subject to an LDP or otherwise restricted; and all are participants in each mortgage transaction.

➤ ___ ___The mortgagee is in compliance with RESPA.

➢ ___ ___Records of QC findings and actions taken are maintained for at least 2 years from the date of insurance endorsement.

➢ ___ ___The reviews are performed within 90 days of loan closing.

➢ ___ ___A minimum of 10% of all rejected loans are reviewed and senior staff concurred with the rejection of the loan.

➢ ___ ___A desk review of the appraisal is conducted on all loans in the QC sampling.

➢ ___ ___An appraisal field review is performed on 10% of the loans in the QC sample.

➢ ___ ___A new credit report is obtained on all loans in the QC sample (using a RMCR, 3-respository merged in-file report, or a business credit report when appropriate)

➢ ___ ___A written re-verification of the mortgagor's employment, deposits, gift letter, alternate credit sources and other sources of funds is obtained.

➢ ___ ___Documents requiring the mortgagor or employee(s) of mortgagee signed signature (other than blanket verification releases) only after completion; and that mortgagor and the employee initial all corrections.

➢ ___ ___If more than one credit report was ordered for a loan file; then all are submitted with the loan package to HUD or the D.E. underwriter.

➢ ___ ___The preliminary loan application, final application and all credit documents are consistent or reconciled.

➢ ___ ___Any outstanding judgments found on the credit report is on the HUD 92900 with an explanation.

➢ ___ ___The file has documentation on source of funds and if other than deposits, the source is verified.

➢ ___ ___If mortgagor is self-employed; the file has a financial statement, tax returns and business credit report.

➢ ___ ___If there is a gift letter, it has the relationship of donor and that the source of funds are acceptable and that any obligation to repay the funds is included on Form HUD-92900 (MCAW).

➢ ___ ___The HUD-1 is accurate and certified.

➢ ___ ___The loan was current when it is submitted for endorsement.

➢ ___ ___It determines whether the mortgagor transferred the property at the time of closing or soon after closing, indicating the possible use of a "straw buyer."

➢ ___ ___All conflicting information is resolved prior to submission to underwriting.

➢ ___ ___There is accurate and complete underwriting.

➢ ___ ___That VOEs, VODs or credit reports are not mishandled by any interested third party or the mortgagor.

➢ ___ ___There are sufficient compensating factors if debt ratios exceed FHA limits.

➢ ___ ___The loan file contains all the required loan processing, underwriting, and legal documents.

➢ ___ ___That the seller did not acquire the property at the time of or soon before closing, indicating a possible property "flip."

➢ ___ ___All conditions are cleared prior to closing.

➢ ___ ___That the mortgagee is in compliance with Fair Lending Laws.

➢ ___ ___That escrow funds are used appropriately.

➢ ___ ___HUD issued reports including underwriting reports and notices of return (regarding cases rejected for insurance due to errors and omissions) are reviewed.

➢ ___ ___Automated underwriting guidelines are followed.

➢ ___ ___Streamline refinances are included in the QC reviews.

Score Yourself

_____ _____ **Total of your answers**

Yes No

How did you do?

You could be a target of Mortgage Fraud if you answered "no" to any questions. It is also an indication that you may have a deficiency in your current pre-funding audit and post-closing quality control plan which your investors, warehouse lenders and HUD require you to maintain an up-to-date Quality Control plan.

Chapter 9:
Buzz Words—What They Say to Get the Fraud Done

"If it is too good to be true...it is probably a fraud."
~ Ron Weber, author of *Information Control and Audit*

As I mentioned earlier in this book, real estate is a people profession. From the real estate agents in the field to the loan processors working with borrowers to the title agents sitting down with families looking to buy their first home, we are people serving people.

Those who would commit fraud know this, perhaps even better than we do...

And, like those of us who are legitimately doing good business in the real estate finance industry, they need people to pull off their scams. What kind of people? Willing people, that's who. People willing to help them lie, people willing to buy shell properties or willing to work for shell corporations or willing to fake facts and figures and forms. They can't do it alone, and more often than not they come to *us* for help.

The sad part is that some of us don't even realize when we're being included in a fraudulent scheme. I believe some of this is partly due to ignorance, other times it's out of laziness, more times than not in the hustle and bustle of our daily lives it's out of sheer busy-ness, but sometimes it's simply due to a "don't ask, don't tell" policy that is quietly eating away at the very integrity of the home financing industry.

Whether we're supervising folks who are helping out these fraudsters or being duped into helping them ourselves, knowing the buzzwords the bad guys use is often our first line of defense in actually ignoring what they have to say.

Here are the most common terms, phrases, and come-ons I've discovered in my considerable research into the subject:

- **"This is done all the time."** Part of a fraudster's ploy is to lure you into believing that what you're doing isn't wrong when, in fact, nothing could be further from the truth. While fraud may get committed every day, that doesn't mean *you* have to be a part of it or, for that matter, tolerate it. Phrases like this one—designed to entice you via the element of conspiracy or convenience—should be a definite red flag as to not only who is committing fraud but, in fact, how they're doing it. Take the first step toward vanquishing fraud in your own private kingdom: report such behavior immediately.

- **"We have never had a problem with it before."** Fraud is an insidious crime. It starts slowly and works its way into the most honest companies, as I witnessed firsthand when fraud was committed right under my nose by a long-time trusted employee. I, too, never had a "problem with it before," i.e. employees committing fraud, until I realized it was too late and HUD shut me down! I once heard someone say that the biggest problems aren't immediately revealed, they're eventually discovered. Just because something hasn't been a problem before doesn't mean it won't be in the future and, most likely, it's a warning sign that this will in fact become a problem before too long. Again, early detection and immediate reportage are the two biggest counter effects for such fraudulent statements.

- **"Can you throw that one away and I will get you a new one?"** Documentation is the means by which fraud is produced. After all, it's the documents that get doctored and the documents that pass without scrutiny by busy or hurried handlers that allows fraud to exist. The forms we use in our industry are nothing short of holy; they are the means and tools by which we borrow and lend. "Throwing one away" is a sure sign that something is amiss, and to combat this all too common practice we should all implement a means of collecting discarded documents, to be reviewed at the end of the day, week, month, or quarter. Much like scientific laboratories have special bins and procedures for destroying biohazard items, we too should treat such requests as "hands off" and, as we should all such statements, report them immediately.

- **"This loan needs to close quickly; it is a super rush."** Time is the ultimate motivator. Why? Because time, after all, is money. Especially in our business, when an increase in the interest rate or public perception that a market is no longer "hot" can mean the difference of thousands, if not tens of thousands, of dollars. This is an old salesmen tactic and while most of us reading it can see its intent a mile away, you'd be surprised by how the right person in the wrong situation can succumb to such an obvious and blatant come-on. After all, it's worked for used car salesmen for as long as, well, there have *been* used car salesmen. Why shouldn't it work in our industry as well?

- **"No one will ever catch us."** Risk may be the ultimate rush, but we've all seen those *World's Dumbest Criminals* shows on TV and the only difference between a bad guy robbing a bank and a bad guy committing fraud is that they usually don't show up on surveillance cameras. And even if they did, it's quite hard to spot someone forging a document when it's just as easy to put down the right figures, as it is to write in the wrong ones. What would we look for, anyway? A phony moustache and sunglasses? A secret decoder ring and trench coat? Well, if we can't always *see* fraud being committed we can certainly *hear* it, and it's important for us to keep our ears open as well as our eyes.

For that matter, let's open our minds as well. Detecting fraud is a mind-set, like exercising or eating right. Habits are born of routine and the surest way to start spotting fraud is to become aware of its existence.

Only then will we start to believe it exists. When we believe in the existence of fraud, we can then start taking active steps, every day, to combat against it. It may be an every day battle, but the longer we fight the stronger we get, and once something becomes a habit the less difficult it is to achieve; and the harder it is to forget.

Like the latest technology the bad guys and gals use to commit fraud (which we'll visit next), fraudsters are always on the cutting edge of criminal vocabulary to get innocent pawns such as you and I to help them commit their crimes. (And never forget, fraud IS a crime!)

Like fashion or pop music, what fraudsters say to dupe us will go in and out of vogue from year to year. Industry terms will change and so, too, will their tactics and terms to keep up with the times. Books like this one, training seminars, workshops, new fraud prevention procedures, websites, newsletters, they can all help to educate us on the various buzz words and phrases to look out for, but we can only combat fraud so far because the bad guys tend to work much harder at this than we do.

Remember: all I'm trying to do with these chapters is to educate you as to the various ways in which the fraudsters do business. Obviously, later books that come out will have tips and strategies the bad guys have adopted since this book's publication, but at the core of this book—and the way in which we'll stop the bad guys—will be the same principles of fraud.

Buzzwords, forms, technologies, interest rates, documents, these will all change, but so too must we to keep up with the latest cons these fraudsters are pulling. That is why you will be able to visit my web site www.preventmortgagefraud.com and I will do my best to keep you up to date on the latest fraudster tactics and schemes. After all, sometimes it's not even what the bad guys are saying, but *how* they say it.

Are you listening?

Chapter 10:
The Age of Electronic Cut & Paste Has Arrived—How the Bad Guys Operate

"A borrower has the right to timely and truthful disclosures regarding the rates and costs of the loan..."

~ From "The Borrower's Bill of Rights,"
www.stopmortgagefraud.com

There's a famous scene in Stephen Spielberg's blockbuster movie *Catch Me if You Can* where Leonardo DiCaprio walks into the bathroom to see a bathtub full of two things: lukewarm water and a fleet of plastic Pan Am airplanes. The water is there to dissolve the glue that holds the real allure for Leo's character: those miniaturized, gummy Pan Am logos on the side of each tiny plastic plane cockpit.

What does Leo do with all those little Pan Am logos? Well, he uses them to affix to blank checks, of course, those blank checks quickly turning into very convincing, if very fake, Pan Am payroll checks.

Ah, the good old days of bank fraud...

Today, of course, fraudsters employ a host of much more sophisticated, but no more complicated, technology to commit fraud. Computers have opened up a whole new world to fraudsters, who use the latest document producing software to make fraudulent pieces of paper that look just like the real thing.

In their ongoing quest to find the latest and the newest technology to commit fraud, the bad guys use:

- **Adobe writer to change documents in adobe formats**: For most of us, Adobe, or .pdf files, are locked little nuggets of information we would never imagine opening up and altering, let alone doctoring for the purposes of committing fraud. However, for an investment of only a few hundred dollars, savvy fraudsters can manipulate .pdf documents to no end. They can change facts, figures, names, addresses, numbers, and any and all forms of information presented in what are supposedly "locked" documents.
- **They use tax return software**: Come spring, two things fill the shelves of local department stores: Easter decorations and tax-return software.

With this second item, the bad guys can create false tax returns for less than $50. (Even less if they wait until after April 15th to buy the software for half price!) Such self-prepared tax documentation is standard operating procedure nowadays, but obviously the opportunity for creating fraudulent documents increases exponentially with every new tax season.

- **They use payroll service software:** Automated payroll deposits, self-produced payroll checks and W-2 forms from small companies, check-writing software and printing paper designed to look just like bank-produced checking documents are a new source of headache for vigilant fraud busters everywhere!

- **They form fake employers:** Those bad guys who have learned that marking "self-employed" is now a huge red flag in the mortgage fraud industry have naturally come up with a clever alternative. Instead of claiming to be self-employed, they simply set up dummy employers for which they don't really work—many of whom don't actually exist! A few hundred dollars can incorporate a company these days, and with an automated answering machine, company letterhead and a few doctored "paychecks," this bad guy or gal is quickly in business.

- **They form fake organizations for anything they are missing:** Today's software comes in so many different flavors a clever criminal can find a way to doctor just about any document, including medical records, employee work files (see above), and other various organizations as far-ranging as civic groups they might have volunteered for or charities they might have donated large amounts of money to. An out-of-service phone number or bounced Email to any of these fraudulent organizations should be a red-flag to alert lenders, but in too many cases the doctored documents for such institutions are "good enough" and it never gets that far. The bad guys know this, and are simply relying on our good will—or busy schedules—to aid in their fraudulent practices.

Of course, technology is always evolving and chances are the fraud schemes will quickly change. Still, it's not the specific documents we're looking out for here, but instead the knowledge that no document, letterhead, logo, form, or figure should be above suspicion.

From tax forms to W-2 forms, company letterhead to letters of recommendation, in today's world it seems nothing is impenetrable to being doctored by the bad guys. Newer, more powerful computers mean bigger ploys. Better software means better-looking documents. Printers are so advanced and so affordable the printing costs that once dissuaded fraudsters are now so economical that forging documents is a no-brainer, literally *and* figuratively.

It seems like a lopsided scale of justice; the bad guys have more and more tools at their disposal and all we have is ourselves. But that's not quite true: we have numbers on our side. There are more of us than there are of them, thank God, and together we can, should, and *will* detect such fraudulent documents with more and more rapidity, skill, and confidence.

Chapter 11:
How Mortgage Fraud Affects ALL Homeowners

"As mortgage industry professionals, we absolutely must take protection of consumer data seriously and ensure that sensitive information does not end up in the hands of fraudsters..."

~ Arthur Prieston, Chairman of the Prieston Group

As we have seen in the last 10 chapters, fraud affects almost everyone in the real estate industry, from the real estate agent to the loan processor, from the owner to the employee, but what about the consumer? How are homeowners—the entire reason for the real estate industry to exist—damaged by mortgage fraud?

Obviously, one can make the case that some homeowners who apply for a mortgage are, in fact, the source of the fraud in the first place. However, the vast majority of people we work with are sincere, motivated, dedicated individuals making one of life's most costly purchases. No matter how sophisticated a homeowner may be in his or her professional life, they are most often baffled by the endless forms, facts, and figures they must face simply to apply for the loan, let alone be approved for it.

It is that process, in fact, that starts the fraud ball rolling. As Arthur Prieston, Chairman of the Prieston Group, states, "Stolen personal information can easily translate into identity theft and potentially fraudulent mortgages in those people's names, a development that is in our best interest to prevent. Yet protecting consumer information is not only good business practice, it is also the law..."

Thus the homeowner is unwittingly the first to allow for fraud, and the last to know about it. We know that fraud exists, we know who most likely perpetrates it and, in fact, the various ways in which they commit fraud. But how is the consumer, how is the potential homeowner, affected?

Reiterates Arthur Prieston, "...consumers pay for the cost of mortgage fraud through increased rates and fees and sometimes through higher property taxes as a result of inflated appraisals. More taxpayer money must be spent to combat this blight, and residents in communities across the country have seen their neighborhoods devastated because of fraud."

Prieston is so right. The cost of fraud may not be felt immediately, but it's there, lurking under the surface and spreading out like pollution to infect millions of innocent homeowners in a variety of ways both seen and unseen.

I know from my personal experience the significant cost that fraud-prevention measures have added to my operational deficit. The price of detecting, reporting, and preventing fraud is not cheap, and there's no doubt some of that cost—albeit as little as possible—eventually gets passed on to the consumer who comes looking for a loan.

Inflated appraisals? Could they really drive up the property taxes in a neighborhood? You bet! If the real estate boom has taught us anything it's that the perception really does become the reality, especially if hyped by the media to the point that people believe popular opinion is the truth.

In fact, if enough fraudulent properties are improperly appraised, the ripple effect is impactful and immediate. And who pays those higher taxes? You, me, and thousands of unwitting homeowners who would never in a million years think of committing real estate fraud.

These significant costs are just the local aftereffects. What about the bigger picture? How about the national level? Many of the quotes I've used throughout this book have come from government officials, be they FBI agents or department heads. You know when the government gets involved in a problem, not only is it big but costly. Someone has to pay those agents to track down fraud, someone has to pay to try all those fraudsters, and if convicted someone has to pay to feed, clothe, and shelter them.

Who? Who will bear the brunt of these costs? Same answer as before: You, me, and thousands of unwitting homeowners who would never in a million years think of committing real estate fraud.

There's no doubt that homeowners pay the price of mortgage fraud. The only way such costs can be avoided is to eliminate, or greatly reduce, the problem. That means you, me, and thousands of unwitting homeowners who would never in a million years think of committing real estate fraud are going to have to start thinking about it, and thinking about it soon.

The faster we can all help prevent fraud, the sooner all of these costs could be reduced, thus saving homeowners and tax payers money…

Epilogue:
The Bottom Line—Fraud IS a Crime!

"Concern about mortgage fraud against our home finance industry has reached such heightened levels that top management of every lender has to decide how they are going to address this growing threat and protect their company, their employees' jobs and the borrowers they serve…"

~ Regina Lowrie, president and chief executive of Gateway Funding Diversified Mortgage Services

Well, here we are. The end of the line. The last stop on the road to fraud detection, prevention, and reportage. The last chapter of the book. So, do you still think my title, *American Epidemic*, is too strong to describe what's going on in the mortgage finance industry as we speak? (I didn't think so.)

I called this chapter *The Bottom Line* because, in the end, that's all that matters: The bottom line. All the information, all the questionnaires and forms and facts and figures don't amount to a hill of beans if you don't remember the bottom line: **Making a false statement to a lender for obtaining a mortgage is a crime.**

Fraud. It's a crime, it's a felony, and as more and more of us become aware of the various red flags, warning signs, and ways to report fraud, fraudsters should and *will* get caught. I know some of you read this book to prevent fraud. I know some of you read it because you've been a victim of fraud. (Heck, I even know that some of you read it because your boss made you!)

I also know that some of you read it to learn what is, or isn't, fraud. Not to learn ways in which to prevent it, but ways in which the law can be skirted, rules can be broken, and the line between morality and profitability crossed.

If you're in this last category I urge you, I beg you: Don't do it. Don't commit fraud. Don't do it on your own because you think no one will notice and don't do it in cahoots with other fraudsters because someone else encourages you to.

I know how easy it can be to get lured into the false perception that fraud isn't *really* a crime; that white-collar criminals *really* "don't count." But it is and, trust me, they do. As the FBI cracks down on fraud, and trust me I only shared with you a small sampling of the hundreds of articles I've read on various cases involving mortgage fraud, penalties are getting stiffer, jail time longer, and fines bigger.

If someone asks you to do something that doesn't seem right, start asking questions and don't stop asking until you are sure you have uncovered the truth. Use the forms I've provided, visit my Website at www.preventmortgagefraud.com, and download the information I've provided there for free. (That's right: FREE!) After all, it's there for a reason; I'm not just doing this all for my own good.

I got lucky. Even though I was the victim of fraud I fought back, and fought back hard, and proved the innocence of not only myself but also my entire company. If I didn't exactly apprehend those who committed fraud against me I at least identified them and, what's more, spread the word in my local real estate community about who they were, where they'd been last and where they were likely to head.

Since then I've become a connoisseur of fraud information. I see it everywhere now; in the paper, the professional journals to which I subscribe, on TV, on the Web. Today I spend as much time writing, publishing, training and speaking about fraud as I do at my "day job." (And I couldn't be happier about that.)

Every day I am able to talk to people just like you and share with them my experience. As unpleasant as it was for me, it can be a cautionary tale for millions of others who might find themselves in the same boat. Hopefully, I can catch them before that boat springs a leak and takes them down the same creek I had to follow. (And, barring that, I can at least offer them a paddle!)

I have become an unlikely advocate for industry-wide changes. Most "fraud busters" come from the outside; government agencies, law enforcement, auditors, etc. But I care enough about my industry to champion this crusade against fraud from the inside out. We need to do this together so that we can prove to HUD and all the others investigating fraud that some lenders are *victims* of fraud, not the perpetrators. In other words, we need to protect ourselves. I was a victim but treated by a lot of people as the cause; now I want to be part of the solution. Case in point: if we all use the information in the book fraud will not succeed.

Crusade. I like that word. After all, as you might have guessed by now, I am a man on a mission. Or, in other words, a **crusade**. I wasn't always this way. For years I lived in a bubble, thinking that mortgage fraud only happened to sloppy, careless, or culpable lenders.

I thought that criminals looked shady, acted obvious, and were stupid. I never imagined fraudsters could look just like you and I. I never thought I'd be outsmarted by someone so willing to do wrong that they'd knowingly ruin the reputation of a company who'd made a living doing right. I've always played it straight with anyone I've ever worked with. I played by the rules and assumed everybody else would, too.

Now I know better, and I want *you* to know better, too...

That's what this book has been about. That's why we've spent this time together. We didn't share a lot of jokes; I didn't teach you how to lose weight or make a million dollars or re-grow your hair. I didn't show you how to flip a house or invest in foreclosures or make big money in a small amount of time. I wrote this book with one intention and you've read it with one intention, and for both of us that was to learn more about mortgage fraud.

I hope I've done my job, and that you've gotten everything out of this book that I offered. Now it's time to do your job. What you do with this information is up to you. I've provided as many resources as I could find at the time of publication and, to provide those that I've run across since the book came out, I've made my website at www.preventmortgagefraud.com freely accessible so that you could go there and get the latest information on fraud prevention straight from a trusted source.

If you still need more help, I'm not hard to find. I'm all over the web and my site has full contact information. If you need another copy of the book for a friend, if you need me to come and train your staff on fraud prevention, if you need help investigating a fraud scheme or if you just want a quick answer to a question that's been nagging at you, feel free to contact me at my website.

I don't ever want you to feel like you're alone in this fight. You've made it this far, we've come a long way together, and there's no way I'd let you down just because the last chapter's done or the book's back on your shelf. I'm here for you, because that's what colleagues do.

I've done my part, but I can only do so much. I would like very much to come to every town and visit every office and chat with every employee and walk you through the various steps you'll need to take to identify, prevent, and report fraud, but if we cannot meet I hope this book and my website can be a suitable alternative.

Bottom line? Preventing mortgage loan fraud begins with you...

Are you ready to do what it takes to start preventing fraud today?

That's what I thought...

Disclaimer:
I Am Not Providing Legal or Other Professional Advice

This book and the contents contained herein have been prepared as a public service and for general informational purposes only. The contents of this book are not intended to provide legal or other professional advice and should not be relied upon as such. Before using or acting upon any Contents on this book, you are advised to seek the advice of your attorney or other appropriate professional to determine: (1) if the Contents apply to your particular circumstances, and (2) the sufficiency of the contents for your unique legal or other needs.

Michael S. Richardson, NexWest Inc. DBA Prevent Mortgage Fraud, and their respective officers, employees and agents are not authorized to practice law on your behalf or to provide you with legal advice. Michael S. Richardson, NexWest Inc. DBA Prevent Mortgage Fraud, expressly disclaim all liability to any person in respect of the consequences of anything done or omitted to be done wholly or partly in reliance upon the use or contents of this web site.

The contents of this book are NOT a substitute for the advice of an attorney. You should seek independent and competent legal counsel before acting (or refraining from acting) upon any of the information contained in this book.

Appendix:

Resource Section

Article for Reprint:
Free for Distribution if Properly Credited

Dear reader,

From time to time "less is more." That is why I've created a 1,500-word article for use in various means of publication throughout the real estate/mortgage lending industry.

To that end, the following article can be used freely in industry newsletters, interoffice memos, and corporate literature as long as printed, as is, with proper attribution to myself as author and with the complete website address in tact. For more information on how to obtain new and original content from either my website or this book, please contact me through my website at www.preventmortgagefraud.com.

Sincerely,

Michael S. Richardson

An American Epidemic:
Mortgage Fraud—a Serious Business

By Michael S. Richardson, www.preventmortgagefraud.com

Would you ever say the "F" word in public? Do you even dare to bring the "F" word up in polite conversation? After all, if you even mention the "F" word it makes any honest, hard working real estate professional quiver. The "F" word is a dirty word in the mortgage industry, and for good reason.

So, have you guessed it yet? What, exactly, IS the "F" word?

"Fraud." More specifically: "Mortgage Fraud."

Don't get me wrong: fraud isn't a factor in every mortgage loan, or even in every branch, but the outcome of even one fraudulent loan gone badly can affect the entire industry, in general, and individual practitioners, in particular.

The ripple effect of fraud is as deep as it is far-reaching. The mortgage lenders and borrowers stand to lose much more than the cost of the damages when fraud appears. At risk is their very reputation in the industry. And as all of us know, in THIS industry our word is our bond; our reputation is our bread and butter.

Who of us, after all, can afford to lose that precious commodity?

Where does mortgage fraud begin and how do we prevent—or at least begin to stop—mortgage fraud? They say timing is everything, and in this case there's never been a better time to commit—or fall prey to—mortgage fraud. The unprecedented real estate boom over the last few years has led to the doubly dangerous refinancing craze currently sweeping the nation.

This one-two double-whammy has sucker-punched its share of lenders and consumers, resulting in widespread appraisal fraud whereby property values are greatly—and unjustifiably—inflated to prey on the unsophisticated buyer who is then left holding the note on a property worth but a fraction of the value at which it had been improperly appraised.

Of course, that's just what happens on the consumer end. How can we, as practitioners working within the industry, control our end of the mortgage fraud equation? Unfortunately, the problem is as internal as it is systemic. The person behind the act usually isn't a professional thief—or even the borrower—it's one or more of—the loan officer, appraiser, real estate agent, and title agent—working together during the mortgage application and approval process. In a large amount of fraud—80 percent by some estimates—it involves an insider...

Is it any wonder? After all, loan originators and their team members have detailed access to the borrower's information in the transaction. From social security numbers to bank account information, it's all above board and on the table. Many of us treat such information as sacrosanct, keeping it under lock and key and using it for one purpose and one purpose only. To those who would perpetrate fraud, however, such information becomes the key they use to unlock the door to fraud.

Every part of the mortgage lending process presents another window of opportunity to unscrupulous loan originators, who by the very nature of their job description come in contact with builders, real estate agents, borrowers, processors, underwriters, appraisers, lender account reps, and title closers.

Each one of these positions or areas needed to get a mortgage leaves an opportunity for fraud!

The *American Epidemic.* Consider that phrase for a moment. Epidemic may sound like a strong word to you, but after considering the latest figures on real estate fraud it is my sincere belief that the word is, in fact, not quite strong enough!

According to the FBI's May 2005 Financial Crimes Report to the Public, the number of mortgage fraud reports filed has escalated nearly 150% since 2003. The report also showed that 80% of the cases involve either overstated property appraisals or non-existent properties.

Fraud. Clearly, the statistics point to nothing short of an epidemic. And yet, really, what do we know about fraud? In point of fact, it's not what we know about fraud that's dangerous; it's what we *don't* know. What's worse is the staggering amount of opportunity with which the American real estate mortgage industry provides those who commit fraud.

According to the Mortgage Bankers of America, or MBA, their 2005 Mortgage Originations Forecast estimates some $2,738,000,000 (that extra trio of zeroes isn't a typo; that's over 2 *trillion* dollars!) in new loans.

This staggering number includes about 20 million in new mortgages required to cover new and existing home sales. Those are big numbers, and now even the MBA is including the likelihood of fraud in their statistics, estimating that 10% to15% of mortgage loans have some kind of fraud involved. This means that between 2 to 3 million home loans originated this year could be fraudulent; that equates to over 7,500 new fraudulent loans *every business day.*

Now, that *is* an epidemic…

Who benefits from such fraud? By my own calculations based on such industry standards, loan officers and others in the mortgage transaction accounted for roughly $8 billion in loan fees and commissions for fraudulent closed loans while real estate agents and real estate companies themselves raked in over $13 billion in commissions from those fraudulent transactions.

The statistics on fraud may be sobering, but what's worse is the sparse amount of stop-gap measures currently in place to prevent this all too common felony.

Many of us come to the industry by way of other careers. With the real estate bubble growing exponentially, and the resulting refinance craze declining with rising interest rates, it is not uncommon for us to be working alongside relative newcomers from diverse careers.

Clearly, the amount of money to be made in real estate—both residential and commercial—lends itself to abuse. New employees mean new training, and lack of new training leads to old mistakes. The growth of fraud is insidious; it creeps up on us, taking us by surprise until, before we know it, someone we work with, someone we work for, or even those who work for us, is committing fraud.

It's so easy, so slick, and until now so largely un-enforced. A number fudged there, a figure left out here, a bogus appraisal, a friend of a friend who plays it fast and loose with a client's verification of rent and a newly scrubbed credit report, and soon enough a mortgage loan is approved, "clear to close," but is in fact fraudulent.

Once a white-collar criminal gets away with it, the process quickly becomes addictive. Success breeds more success, and before long such crafters of fraudulent mortgage loans clearly begin feeling that not only are they above the law but, in fact, they aren't doing anything wrong in the first place.

But those of us who take our profession seriously, who are in this business to help sincere, hardworking, law-abiding citizens obtain housing in a fair market for a mortgage that works for them can think of little worse than those who prey on the innocent, the righteous, the unsophisticated and the trusting.

Fraud can happen to anyone: employees, buyers, sellers, investors, and owners. It can happen anywhere: big cities, small towns, storied and well-recognized firms and smaller mom and pop businesses who just want to do the right thing.

So, who still thinks "epidemic" is too harsh a word?!?

Don't let the statistics get you down: according to the Mortgage Bankers Association of America, "…the U.S. Attorney and others have suggested that as much as 70–80 percent of mortgage fraud can be avoided through aggressive fraud awareness and detection efforts."

That's where I come in: being recently appointed the Managing Director at Risk Mitigation as a specialist in preventing mortgage fraud, as well as my personal experiences with mortgage fraud, have given me a doctoral degree from the school of hard knocks. Much like you, I "never thought it could happen to me."

But it did.

It can.

And if the statistics prove out, it probably will…

But it doesn't have to. Not to you, anyway. And not to those you do business with, not if you obtain all the tools you'll need to prevent yourself from becoming a victim of this increasingly common crime.

Prevention Forms for YOUR Company

On the following pages are the various forms I use to indoctrinate new as well as old loan managers, debt handlers, clerks, etc. I stress I'm no lawyer, but these forms have been cleared by my attorney and should be of great use to you as you begin to build your own internal checks and balances system. And remember, updates and changes will always be available at my website, if you'd prefer to download this information instead of photocopy. Here goes:

Your Mortgage Company USA
Appraisal Policy Statement

Purpose: Your Mortgage Company USA provides real estate financing for the communities in which it operates. Major importance is placed on making economical, non-discriminatory home mortgages available for the residents of these communities. Quality originations of real estate home mortgages are critical to the stability and predictability of earnings for Your Mortgage Company USA. Maintenance of quality loan originations depends upon various elements of sound underwriting of which quality real estate appraisals are a vital element.

Statement of Policy: All appraisals prepared for Your Mortgage Company USA must at a minimum:

- Comply with the standards of the Uniform Standards of Professional Appraisal Practice (USPAP), promulgated by the Appraisal Standards Board of the Appraisal Foundation, located at 1029 Vermont Ave., NW, Washington DC, 20005.
- Be written and contain sufficient information and analysis to support the decision to engage in the transaction.
- Be based upon the definition of market value as set forth in the USPAP.
- Be performed by a State licensed or certified appraiser.

It is against Your Mortgage Company USA policy to discriminate against a loan applicant or borrower because of race, color, religion, national origin, sex, marital status, handicap, familial status or age, the fact that all or part of an applicant's income comes from any public assistance program or because the applicant has exercised any right under the Consumer Protection Act or any similar state law. The policy will be periodically reviewed and amended by the Board of Directors as necessary.

Management Directive: *The Board of Directors directs management to develop procedures to implement this policy and demonstrate their effectiveness in ensuring compliance.*

I have read, understand and will abide by Your Mortgage Company USA
Appraisal Policy Statement

Loan Officer/Loan Coordinator/Processor

By: _____

Date: _____

Printed Name: _____

Title: _____

Loan Officer Responsibilities and Guidelines
Company:
Goals

- Always return borrower and realtor calls in a timely fashion, whether it is with good news and/or challenging news.
- Always keep borrower and realtor informed of what stage the loan is currently in, processing, underwriting, closing, etc.
- Have all loans pre-approved by DU/LP or try to find a manual underwrite within 72-hours of application. We want to take as many surprises out of the loan process as possible.
- Have all loans completely approved and closing package shipped to title company/closing agent no later than 72 hours before the pre-set closing date.

Essential Functions of Loan Officer

- Acts as liaison between the real estate agents, applicants and processor.
- Conducts telephone or face-to-face conversations with customers concerning the loan application for residential real estate purchase or refinance loans.
- Needs to have a thorough understanding of basic loan programs (Conventional [FNMA/FHLMC], FHA and VA) offered our approved investors, and is able to explain these to applicants. You can find the guidelines for all of the loans listed on the daily rate sheets via the investor web pages in most cases. It would be a good practice to include a copy of guidelines or loan matrix in each loan package for processor on the loan program the borrower has chosen, highlighting out of the ordinary issues for them to see or watch for.
- Pre-qualify every applicant by performing loan amount, income and credit calculations in accordance to loan programs offered by our investors and/ or specifically requested by applicant. We will always try to pull a single file credit report for pre-quals unless we are most certain we have the loan.
- Explain to applicants the different loan programs provided by our investors, and assist the applicant in finding the correct program for their needs. If the loan officer needs help choosing a loan product with challenging files they need to ask operation managers with different investors or the local reps, and or underwriters, but it is the loan officer's job to qualify and sell the product to borrowers.
- Prepares applications, gathers information from the applicants, and assists applicants in completing loan applications. Also to keep loan application in compliance with all HUD and company regulations.
- The upfront fees are the loan officer's responsibility, but the LO has the choice of not collecting up front. If for any reason the loan does not close and Your Mortgage Company USA orders appraisal and credit, Your Mortgage Company USA may deduct from future commissions for the out of pocket costs. This will be handled on a case-by-case basis. Please deliver checks to Your Mortgage Company USA.
- Enters the loan application in Point, prepares and mails disclosures to applicant within 3 days of the date the loan officer completes the application with the applicants (as required by Federal Regulations X and Z), orders tri-merge credit report and places file in proper order for processing and underwriting.

- Completes Rate Locks as necessary. This is a very critical area for the borrower and LO, if a LO asks an operations staff member to lock a loan they take the chance of not getting it done correctly and potentially causing a loss for the borrower, LO and Your Mortgage Company USA.
- Loan coordinators/processors will help with completion of loan application, setting appointments, returning calls, calling out conditions and marketing as requested by the loan officer.
- Loan officer will be responsible for scheduling a timely meeting with the assigned processor to review any and all issues for the LO's whole pipeline. This will help keep the loan files moving quickly and smoothly during loan process and eliminate any potential surprises or delays in closing loans. It can then be determined who is going to make additional contact or order additional information needed from borrower, realtor or third party vendors.

Upon Receipt of Loan Application

When receiving the loan application package from the borrower (on an application that was completed by mail), the loan officer must review the application to ensure that the application and disclosures were signed and completed with the minimal required information, as follows—Totally Complete Uniform Residential Loan Application (FNMA1003) must be completed, signed and dated by at least one borrower and by the loan officer within three days of application, and the following information must be furnished:

- Employment history for the most recent 2 years (24 months). List employer name, address and company phone number (manager cell phone number is not acceptable).
- Landlords for the most recent 2 years (24 months). List name of landlord (or name of apartment complex) address and phone number.
- Current mortgage company name, account number, approximate balance and monthly payment for all mortgage loans that closed in the most recent 24 months.
- Name and complete account number for each open credit/liability account (usually 13 or 16 digits except AMEX at 15 digits). Please include Creditor name (i.e.: "Citibank Visa," not just "Visa").
- Name, type of account and account number for asset accounts (checking, savings, 401K's, money market, etc.).

Make sure the application is signed and dated by borrower. The application must be signed and dated by at least one borrower before Your Mortgage Company USA, LLC can process the loan request.

Special Note:
The Loan Officer must sign and date application and origination check list

- Borrower has provided all supporting documentation.
- Three-bureau merged in-file credit report.
- The most recent 30 days pay stubs. Pay stub must disclose YTD information.
- W2's for the last two years.

- The most recent statement of each liquid asset (money markets, stocks, bonds, pensions, CD's, checking, savings, etc.)
- Bankruptcy papers, divorce decrees and child support documentation when necessary.
- Written explanations for any gaps in employment, changes in employment explaining correlation between jobs, credit problems, late pays, bankruptcy, judgments, and credit inquiries. If the borrower did not provide any of the documentation required, loan officer must call borrower and request the missing documentation before submitting the application package to underwriter. Loan officer must note that the phone call and request was made on the conversation log. If the applicants do not provide sufficient information for the underwriter to make a credit decision, the loan file will be suspended.

Disclosures and Regulations Needed by Law

Federal Regulations require all applications accepted by any representative of Your Mortgage Company USA be subject to the following:

- Truth-In-lending (TIL);
- Good Faith Estimate (GFE);
- Provider of Services Disclosure;
- Adjustable Rate Mortgage Disclosure, Servicing Disclosure Statement;
- Borrower's Certification and Authorization to Release Information;
- Fair Lending Notice;
- ECOA;
- Notice to Homeowner—FHA Assumption Disclosures (FHA);
- Importance of Home Inspection (FHA);
- Important Notice to Homebuyers—HUD 92900;
- Booklet of Settlement Charges;
- All other appropriate documents and/or disclosures…

These regulations require the disclosures be provided (prepared and mailed) within three business days after the application is received or prepared.

The Provider of Services Disclosure must show all required service provider names such as credit reporting agency, appraiser, flood determination company, etc., their addresses and phone numbers.

Good Faith Estimate of Settlement Charges
(Regulation X - RESPA)

A loan officer is required to provide the loan applicant with a Good Faith Estimate for each settlement charge which will be listed in Section L of the Uniform Settlement Statement (HUD-1). Any changes should be made by the LO, but a processor should help in this process as needed.

The loan officer shall supply a typed Good Faith Estimate, signed and dated by Loan Officer, to the applicant(s) (buyers) and the sellers (if they are paying any closing costs) within three business days after the application is received or prepared.

The Good Faith Estimate (GFE) should reflect all known costs. If costs are not paid by the applicant (borrower), they still must be disclosed on the GFE with the entity shown who is responsible for the fees. All fees which are paid outside of closing of the loan (for example, appraisal and credit report) are considered "POC" or paid outside of closing. They must be marked "POC" and the fee should be shown outside the borrower estimated fee column. On "No point—No fee" loan, the fees paid to third party vendors such as tax service, appraisal, credit report, flood, etc. must be shown as "POC" on the GFE. Any fee paid by the Loan Officer or MAM must be reflected as "PBL" (Paid by Lender).

Truth-In-Lending Act
(Regulation Z - TIL)

The Truth-In-Lending disclosure should reflect all costs considered in the pre-paid finance charge. The loan officer shall supply the Truth-In-Lending to the applicant(s) within three business days after the application is received or prepared.

Evidence Loan File Is In Compliance With Federal Regulations

To evidence compliance with Federal Regulations, the loan file must contain:

- An application signed and dated by borrowers (at least one borrower's signature is required) and the application to be signed and dated by the loan officer and/or assistant.
- FHA/VA Addendums to the application on all government loans.
- A copy of the Good Faith Estimate that was prepared for and signed by, or mailed to, the applicant(s) within three business days after the application is received or prepared.
- Provider of Services Disclosure that was signed by, or mailed to the applicant(s) within three business days after the application is received or prepared.
- A copy of the Truth-In-Lending that was prepared for, and signed by, or mailed to the applicant(s) within three business days after the application is received or prepared.
- A copy of the Servicing Disclosure Statement that was signed by, or mailed to the applicant(s) within three business days after the application is received or prepared.
- Adjustable Rate Mortgage Disclosure that was signed by, or mailed to the applicant(s) within three business days after the application is received or prepared.
- Borrower's Certification and Authorization to Release Information.
- Fair Lending Notice that was signed by, or mailed to the applicant(s) within three business days after the application is received or prepared.
- ECOA Notice that was signed by, or mailed to the applicant(s) within three business days after the application is received or prepared.
- Notice to Homeowner—FHA Assumption Disclosures (HUD) that was signed by, or mailed to the applicant(s) within three business days after the application is received or prepared.
- Importance of Home Inspection (HUD) that was signed by, or mailed to the applicant(s) within three business days after the application is received or prepared.

- Important Notice to Homebuyers—HUD 92900 that was signed by, or mailed to the applicant(s) within three business days after the application is received or prepared.
- Lead Based Paint disclosure on government loans.

Important Note:

The application and all disclosures are borrower and property specific. On a "pre-qual" or "TBD" where a property has not been selected, the loan officer will be required to completely re-disclose when the borrowers locate the property they want to purchase and provide the loan officer with a copy of the purchase contract.

The Patriot Act:
Section 326 of the USA PATRIOT Act Requires a Customer Identification Program

Effective October 1, 2005, your originators must submit the following information on all applicants and co-applicants before you should process any credit applications.

1. Customer's Full Name.
2. Customer's Physical Street Address.
3. Customer's Date of Birth.
4. Customer's Social Security Number.

You need to inform your originators, and they should acknowledge that they are required to provide notification to all applicants to comply with the provisions of the USA PATRIOT Act and to provide the identifying information as requested to complete the processing of all loan applications.

Per the Customer Identification Program, the following notice MUST be given to all Applicants:

IMPORTANT INFORMATION ABOUT PROCEDURES:

To help the government fight the funding of terrorism and money laundering activities, Federal law requires all financial institutions to obtain, verify, and record information that identifies each person who opens an account.

What This Means for You:

When you apply for a new loan, we will ask for your name, address, date of birth, and other information that will allow us to identify you. We may also ask to see your driver's license or other identifying documents.

Miscellaneous Notes

All documentation in file must be completed in ink. Any documentation completed in pencil will be unacceptable.

Application Review

- Underwriters will only accept complete application packages for underwriting. It will be the processor's job to gather the rest of the documentation needed to deem application package complete and return the application package to the underwriter.
- An incomplete application package could be returned to the loan officer depending on the relationship the LO has with underwriter as the LO and underwriter should work out an amicable working relationship for completing loan files.
- All loans not approved immediately by DU/LP should be submitted for pre-underwriting to ensure quality and timely processing.

Preparing the File for Processing and Underwriting

The processor prepares the loan application file for submission to underwriting as soon as possible after receiving loan package from loan officer or after receiving the loan package from the applicant in the case of a "by mail" application. The loan application must be signed and dated by loan officer when submitted to processing.

The loan officer and/or assistant prepares the file for processing by performing the following duties:

- Enter application in POINT and inform the processor.
- Print 1003 and MCAW/VA Loan Analysis/1008.
- Prepare disclosures and mail them to appropriate parties (when applicable).
- Prepare FNMA-1003 (Uniform Residential Loan Application) and FHA/VA Addendums when applicable.
- Good Faith Estimate—complete and mail to applicant and seller within three business days after the application is received or prepared. Good Faith Estimate figures must match figures on Uniform Residential Loan Application (Loan Amount, Interest Rate, Term, and Details of Transaction).
- Provider of Services Disclosure (Good Faith Estimate Addendum).
- Truth-In-Lending—completed and mailed to the applicant within three business days after the application is received or prepared. Truth-In-Lending figures must match figures on Uniform Residential Loan Application
- Adjustable Rate Mortgage Disclosure—completed with worse case adjustable payment amount changes (increases) listed for term of loan.
- Servicing Disclosure Statement.
- Borrower's Certification and Authorization to Release Information.
- Fair Lending Notice.
- ECOA.
- Notice to Homeowner—FHA Assumption Disclosures (FHA).
- Importance of Home Inspection (FHA).
- Important Notice to Homebuyers—HUD 92900.
- All other appropriate documents and/or disclosures…

Additional Items for the Processor

- Place file in specific processing order according to underwriter needs for each loan product.
- Make copies of any checks provided and place a copy and the original in file. Deliver checks to Your Mortgage Company USA or designated employee.
- Be aware of where the loan will be underwritten and how many days that investor is at with underwriting, as certain loans will have to go out of state and you should plan on 3 extra days for underwriting to go out of state.

Deliver file to Investor/Underwriter

I have read, understand and will abide by Your Mortgage Company USA
Loan Officer Responsibilities and Guidelines

Loan Officer

By:_____

Date:_____

Printed Name:_____

Title:_____

Some of these guidelines or fees could change without notice, based on HUD regulations or changing policies, we will do our best to inform you as soon as we know.

Your Mortgage Company USA
Mortgage Loan Origination Agreement

These are the rules and agreement by and between Your Mortgage Company USA and all Originators. From time to time, the ORIGINATOR intends to enter into binding commitments for the delivery of applications at a future date of Mortgage Loans. Each loan shall be processed and closed by Your Mortgage Company USA and, ORIGINATOR hereby agrees that the following terms and conditions will govern and form a part of all such commitments unless specifically altered or modified in writing, approved, and signed by Your Mortgage Company USA and ORIGINATOR. Your Mortgage Company USA may sell such loans in the secondary market ("Investor").

1. ELIGIBLE LOANS:
   For the purpose of this Agreement, the following mortgages shall be deemed "eligible mortgages" for applications from ORIGINATOR.
   A. The mortgage or deed of trust must be a valid first lien.
   B. Each loan must meet requirements by Your Mortgage Company USA Mortgage LLC, Investors, FNMA, and FHLMC & FHA/VA.
   C. The maximum loan amount cannot exceed limits set by FNMA, FHLMC, FHA/VA and Investors, or Your Mortgage Company USA.
   D. All eligible programs that Your Mortgage Company USA and Your Mortgage Company USA will provide applicable program manuals to the ORIGINATOR.

2. PRICE OF LOANS AND INTEREST RATES:
   Prices and eligible programs will be announced daily by YOUR MORTGAGE COMPANY USA and the individual investors YOUR MORTGAGE COMPANY USA is approved to do business with and reserves the right to change prices during the day or to refuse to accept registrations if the terms do not reflect current pricing.

3. ORIGINATOR REPRESENTS AND WARRANTS THAT:
   A. It is the sole owner of the mortgage loan application and has authority to originate, transfer, and assign same on the terms herein set forth; there has been no sale, assignment, or hypothecation thereof by ORIGINATOR.
   B. ORIGINATOR complies fully with all applicable federal, state, and local statutes including, but not limited to, the Federal Truth-in-Lending Act, the Real Estate Settlement Procedures Act, the Equal Credit Opportunity

Act, HUD, GNMA, FNMA, FHLMC, and specific Investor regulations, requirements, and procedures in existence at time of origination.

C. There are no material misrepresentations of the mortgagee or originator in the making of the mortgage loan application.

E. ORIGINATOR agrees that the complete mortgage loan application shall begin or hand over file to assigned processor for processing by the end of the next business day following the day such application is taken by ORIGINATOR.

F. Services to be performed by the ORIGINATOR in conjunction with the origination of eligible loans:

1) Complete the application according to Exhibit A attached with information from the applicant(s).

2) Obtain from the applicant(s) an executed authorization to release application and related information.

3) Calculate loan-to-value and debt-to-income ratios to pre-qualify the applicant(s).

4) Educate and counsel applicants as to loan program characteristics and costs.

5) Obtain and review credit report with applicant(s)

6) Collect financial information from applicants.

7) Order property inspections where applicable.

8) Provide all applicable program disclosures.

9) Provide problem solving assistance to applicant(s).

10) Maintain contact with the applicants, realtors, and others involved in the transactions between applications and closing.

G. As total compensation for such services, ORIGINATOR shall receive as agreed on all closed loans. This fee shall be payable within a reasonable time after the closing of the loan. It is subject to change as needed and agreed.

4. YOUR MORTGAGE COMPANY USA REPRESENTS AND WARRANTS THAT:

A. Upon receipt of a mortgage application that has been registered and completed in accordance with the agreement and all applicable laws and regulations it will process and close the loan in a timely manner and in accordance with established secondary market guidelines.

Such processing by YOUR MORTGAGE COMPANY USA shall only include and be limited to:

1) Complete and send to the applicant, within three (3) business days, based solely upon the information supplied by the ORIGINATOR, unless the originator has already completed the following disclo-

sures: YOUR MORTGAGE COMPANY USA is to complete and send Items (i) through (v).

(i) Good Faith Estimate of closing costs;

(ii) Servicing Transfer Disclosure;

(iii)Interest Rate and Loan Point Agreement;

(iv) Truth-in-Lending Disclosure; and,

(v) Any other disclosures required by applicable laws.

2) Prepare and mail Verification of Deposit and Verification of Employment to the source of funds and the applicant's employer.

3) Order the appropriate appraisals and title policy.

4) Submit the completed loan package to underwriting for approval.

5) Prepare all necessary closing documents.

6) Work with the title company to clear any title exceptions that may occur after closing.

B. The required disclosures will be prepared and mailed to the applicant(s) within three (3) business days of receipt of application from ORIGINATOR.

C. Each loan will be underwritten in accordance with established secondary market guidelines and specific Investor requirements.

D. The loan closing documentation will be prepared and delivered to the closing attorney or title company.

E. The loan applications provided to ORIGINATOR by YOUR MORTGAGE COMPANY USA shall comply fully with all applicable federal, state, and local statutes including, but not limited to, the Federal Truth-In-Lending Act, the Real Estate Settlement Procedures Act, the Equal Credit Opportunity Act, HUD, GNMA, FNMA, FHLMC, and specific Investor regulations, requirements, and procedures in existence at time of origination. YOUR MORTGAGE COMPANY USA shall be required to update these forms as updated on a uniform basis.

5. CERTIFICATION RELATING TO KICKBACKS:

YOUR MORTGAGE COMPANY USA and ORIGINATOR hereby certify that they have not and will not receive any fees or considerations of any types, directly or indirectly, from any party in connection with any transaction, except the fees that will be fully disclosed on the loan settlement statement for each transaction which will be in accordance with all laws and RESPA regulations.

6. SOLICITATION FOR REFINANCE:

ORIGINATOR agrees that neither ORIGINATOR nor any employee, agent, or contractor of ORIGINATOR shall knowingly solicit for mortgage refinance any mortgage loan, which is or could be construed to be subject to a commitment or to this Agreement. If ORIGINATOR knowingly solicits, ORIGINATOR agrees to repay YOUR MORTGAGE COMPANY USA for any fees received for the origination of the refinanced loan(s).

7. REPURCHASE AGREEMENT:

ORIGINATOR agrees that if a loan is considered unacceptable by Your Mortgage Company USA (including fraud or misrepresentation) or fails to meet the ORIGINATOR'S representation, warranties, or any other covenants set forth in this Agreement, ORIGINATOR will repurchase said loan within ten (10) business days of written notice from YOUR MORTGAGE COMPANY USA. ORIGINATOR will repurchase said loan at a repurchase price equal to par price paid by YOUR MORTGAGE COMPANY USA plus any interest, late charges, advances, premiums, service-release premiums, and any loss or expense (including any reasonable attorney fees) which YOUR MORTGAGE COMPANY USA shall incur as a result of this loan.

8. TAX SERVICES:

All loans MUST have a tax contract in effect through a firm designated by YOUR MORTGAGE COMPANY USA.

9. FUNDING:

All loans will be closed with the approval of YOUR MORTGAGE COMPANY USA and in the name of YOUR MORTGAGE COMPANY USA or the individual investor as required.

10. LOAN FALLOUT/CANCELLATION:

ORIGINATOR agrees to keep loan fallout/cancellation rate below 25%. A rate higher than 35% could result in the assessment of a penalty against ORIGINATOR (as determined by YOUR MORTGAGE COMPANY USA in its sole discretion) and/or cancellation of this Agreement.

11. CANCELLATION:

ORIGINATOR agrees and acknowledges that in the event it breaches or is otherwise not in compliance with any terms or provisions of this Agreement (including, but not limited to, any failure by ORIGINATOR to pay reasonable losses, fees, or penalties assessed by YOUR MORTGAGE COMPANY USA thereunder), then YOUR MORTGAGE COMPANY USA will upon written notice to ORIGINATOR and after having provided ORIGINATOR five (5) calendar days within which to cure such breach, cancel this Agreement and hereby rescind its obligation to fund any mortgage loans not registered with the YOUR MORTGAGE COMPANY USA system as of the receipt date of written notice.

13. FURTHER CONDITIONS:
   A. ORIGINATOR agrees that the failure of YOUR MORTGAGE COMPANY USA to enforce any condition of this Agreement as to any mortgage loan is not a waiver of that or any other condition with regard to that or any other loan under this Agreement.
   B. ORIGINATOR'S repudiation, breach, or inability to perform any of its commitment(s) shall be deemed a repudiation, breach, or failure to perform all of its outstanding commitments to YOUR MORTGAGE COMPANY USA.
   C. This Agreement or any commitments entered into in accordance with this Agreement are not assignable by ORIGINATOR. They may be assigned by YOUR MORTGAGE COMPANY USA without notice to ORIGINATOR.
   D. ORIGINATOR will be qualified to do business in all jurisdictions where its business requires and obtain and retain all necessary licenses to do its business.
   ORIGINATOR also agrees to notify YOUR MORTGAGE COMPANY USA should any material change occur to the condition of Originator's loans that may affect YOUR MORTGAGE COMPANY USA. It is further understood, should any material adverse changes occur, YOUR MORTGAGE COMPANY USA has the right to limit receipt of any applications from ORIGINATOR to YOUR MORTGAGE COMPANY USA.
   E. The terms and conditions of this Agreement shall be construed and governed by the laws of the state of Colorado.
   F. Time is of the essence with respect to each and every provision of these standard terms and conditions and commitments entered into according to this Agreement.

I have read, understand and will abide by Your Mortgage Company USA Mortgage Loan Origination Agreement

Loan Officer/Loan Coordinator/Processor

By:_____

Date:_____

Printed Name:_____

Title:_____

Loan Coordinator & Processor Responsibilities

Essential Functions

The loan coordinator/processor is responsible for processing loan application files to ensure that they contain <u>all</u> the supporting documentation the underwriter will need to arrive at a <u>final</u> credit decision. This includes the review of all documentation for completeness and accuracy, identifying additional items required, and properly organizing the documents in the loan file.

The processor must ensure all documentation in file will satisfy company, governmental agency and investor requirements. The loan coordinator/processor also ensures adherence to regulations.

Types of Mortgage Loans

The loan coordinator/processor will be required to process different types of mortgage loans and loan programs to include, but not limited to the following:

- FHA
- VA
- Conventional (FNMA, FHLMC and Private Investors)
- Jumbo

Workloads and Processing Timeframes

The loan coordinator/processor will be expected to process 20 loans consistently every month, and be able to close 12 to 15 loans monthly. (With an assistant, the Loan coordinator/processor will be required to process 30 loans consistently every month, and be able to close 15 to 20 loans monthly.)

Initial File Review/Additional Information Request

To ensure compliance with ECOA (Regulation B), the loan coordinator/processor is responsible for notifying the applicant(s) within a specific period of time from the receipt of the loan application, of any additional credit items or documentation needed to complete the loan application. This notification is known as *Request for Additional Information* and it is to be issued within 48 hours upon receipt of loan application by the loan coordinator/processor.

The loan coordinator/processor sends a *Request for Additional Information* to the applicant(s) and indicates any documentation necessary to complete the loan application.

Truth-In-Lending/Good Faith Estimate

The loan coordinator/processor verifies that a copy of the Truth-In-Lending and Good Faith Estimate are in the file and were prepared within 3 days of receipt of loan application. If not, they are required to inform the loan officer to aid in producing documents and provide to applicants within 3 days of receipt of application. The initial Truth-In-Lending Statement and Good Faith Estimate do not need to be signed by all applicants, but will require a minimum of one signature.

Complete Applications

The loan coordinator/processor will ensure that a decision regarding the loan application is issued within 3 business days of receipt of a completed application package by following applicant notification requirements regarding required information, credit items, or documentation during the processing period.

Appraisals

The loan coordinator/processor will notify the loan officer, selling agent and listing agents of the appraised value and any appraisal conditions the same day the appraisal is received. When the appraisal conditions have been satisfied, the loan coordinator/processor will be responsible for ordering an inspection. It is the responsibility of the loan coordinator/processor to follow-up with the listing agent on the completion of the appraisal conditions.

Submitting the Application

When all required documentation, has been obtained, and the loan application file is complete and ready for submission to underwriting for final approval, the loan coordinator/processor will ensure all information in computer system is accurate and complete.

When the loan application file is received in the Underwriting Department, it is reviewed by an underwriter who will determine the final credit decision.

Final Process After Approval

Upon receipt of the approved loan application file, the loan coordinator/processor will perform the following tasks:

- Review loan application file to validate all information on the computer system and updates any changed information prior to loan closing (this includes loan terms, appraisal, underwriting calculations per MCAW, VA Loan Analysis, or Transmittal Summary and the loan approval information).

- Review rate lock terms and verify against approval terms.
- Coordinate completion of loan application package by communicating with the loan officer and the applicant, advising all parties of final loan approval, "prior to closing" (PTC) and/or "at time of closing" (ATC) conditions.
- Coordinate the loan closing and document order time frames with the loan officer, the applicant and the settlement agent.
- Prepare loan for closing and deliver loan to closing department at least 48 hours before scheduled closing date and time.

Incomplete Applications/Inactive Files/Notice of Incompleteness

On or before the twenty-fifth (25 days) of receipt of the application by the company a *Request for Additional Information* form must be send to the applicants, if, in fact, the applicants had not complied to the *Request for Additional Information* sent at the beginning of loan process. The notice of incompleteness provides a specific period of time to the applicant to provide all documentation necessary to make a credit decision or the file WILL be canceled for incompleteness. The letter must be sent before the Regulation "B" requirement of notice of incompleteness within 30 days of receipt of application (if the application is still incomplete).

Since the applicant has already received a *Request for Additional Information*, the loan coordinator/processor may already know the circumstances of the applicant. The *Request for Additional Information* can be sent at any time prior to 30 days of receipt of application. The *Request for Additional Information* expiration date should be 5 days (but could be any reasonable date, if requested by the borrower, which will allow the applicant to complete the application).

After the time frames have been exhausted for attempting to obtain outstanding documentation, the applicant does not respond, and the loan application remains incomplete, the file can be immediately canceled for incompleteness. The loan file is documented and delivered to loan officer. Loan officer will follow "Adverse Action" procedures.

If the applicant provides the information or documentation within the time period specified; the loan coordinator/processor continues to process the loan.

Withdrawn Application

When the loan coordinator/processor is informed that the applicant wishes to withdraw their application, the information concerning the withdrawal must be entered in the comments log.

The applicant may withdraw their loan application without disclosing the reason for doing so.

The applicant may withdraw due to unwillingness to provide requested information, or he/she may be dissatisfied with the loan amount Your Mortgage Company USA, LLC is willing to provide. If this is the case, the withdrawal is considered to be a decline <u>not a withdrawal</u>, and an adverse action letter must be sent.

HMDA Information

The Processor will ensure that the HMDA information in Point, is correct on all loan applications for reporting purposes. The following information must be verified:

- Gender   Occupancy Code
- Race   State Code
- Marital Status   County Code
- Gross Annual Combined Income from 1008, Date Application Signed
- Property Address, Loan Amount to nearest $1,000

The required information must be correct when entered in Point. The information must also be verified throughout the loan process to ensure that any new or revised information is updated.

HMDA information cannot be obtained from the loan application for the following:

- Monthly Income used to qualify borrower as determined by underwriter.
- Census tract information which is verified with the appraisal when the appraisal is received or with the flood certification.
- The MSA code which is determined based upon the area in which the property is located (usually county area).

Quality Control (Also see Quality Control Plan Document)

- Initial Uniform Residential Loan Application (FNMA 1003), initial Good Faith Estimate of Settlement Costs and initial Truth-In-Lending Disclosure, must all agree (be the same loan program, loan amount, term, rate, property address, etc.).
- All corrections to documents must be initialed by the person completing forms.
- Any "Verifications" (such as VOE's, VOD's, VOM's, VOR's, etc.) may not be handled by any *interested* third party (example: YOUR MORTGAGE

COMPANY USA employees, borrowers, co-borrowers, relatives, etc.). Accepted methods of delivery are: 1) US Postal Service, UPS, FedEx, Airborne, faxed etc., or 2) Outside courier service. All verifications must be signed by a YOUR MORTGAGE COMPANY USA employee.

- <u>All</u> credit reports ordered and/or received must be included in loan package. This is to include <u>all</u> supplements received.
- Original application may never be altered in any way or at any time after applicants have signed it.
- The preliminary loan application must list each outstanding liability and each asset of the borrower that was used to qualify for the mortgage. If any liability or asset is missing from the original loan application the borrower must submit a written explanation of why these were not included in the original loan application and were not disclosed.
- If self-employed, the file must contain financial statements. There are times that a business credit report must also be included (review your manuals/guidelines to determine when these are needed).
- Thermal fax paper is unacceptable.

Other Loan Coordinator/Processor Duties

- Process mail daily, updating system and file. Review items for accuracy prior to adding to file.
- Maintain communication with applicant and loan officer of current loan status.
- Voice mail/Phone messages/E-mails to be returned as soon as possible.
- Desks and work areas are to be kept clean and organized.

I have read, understand and will abide by Your Mortgage Company USA
Loan Coordinator and Processor Responsibilities Document

Loan Coordinator/Processor

By:_____

Date:_____

Printed Name:_____

Title:_____

Loan Fraud
Zero Tolerance Statement

All Your Mortgage Company USA loan officers, loan coordinators and processors must be aware that they bear the responsibility of all incidents of fraud for loans originated by Your Mortgage Company USA The loan officer, loan coordinator and/or processor is responsible for the content and quality of each application taken and each loan submitted to our investors.

THE SUBMISSION OF A LOAN APPLICATION CONTAINING FALSE INFORMATION IS A CRIME!

Types of Loan Fraud

1. Submission of inaccurate information, including false statements on loan application(s) and falsification of documents purporting to substantiate credit, employment, deposit and asset information, personal information including identity, ownership/non-ownership of real property, etc.
2. Forgery of partially or predominantly accurate information.
3. Incorrect statements regarding current occupancy or intent to maintain minimum continuing occupancy as stated in the security instrument.
4. Lack of due diligence by loan officer, loan coordinator and/or processor, including failure to obtain all information required by the application and failure to request further information as dictated by borrower's responses to other questions.
5. Unquestioned acceptance of information or documentation which is known, should be known, or should be suspected to be inaccurate.
   a. Simultaneous or consecutive processing of multiple owner-occupied loans from one applicant supplying different information on each application.
   b. Allowing an applicant or interested third-party to "assist with the processing of the loan."
6. Loan officer's, loan coordinator's and/or processor's non-disclosure of relevant information.

Consequences

The effects of loan fraud are costly to all parties involved. Your Mortgage Company USA stands behind the quality of its loan production. Fraudulent loans damage our reputation with our investors and mortgage insurance providers.

Consequences to Loan Officer, Loan Coordinator and/or Processor

1. Loss of employment.
2. Criminal Prosecution.
3. Civil action and employment termination by Your Mortgage Company USA
4. Civil action by applicant/borrower or other parties to the transaction
5. Loss of professional license, if any.

Consequences to Borrower

1. Acceleration of debt (FNMA/FHLMC Mortgage/Deed of Trust. Item #6 states: "Borrower shall also be in default if Borrower, during the loan application process, gave materially false or inaccurate information or statements to lender (or failed to provide lender with any material information) in connection with the loan evidenced by the Note, including, but not limited to, representations concerning Borrower's occupancy of the property as a principal residence."
2. Criminal prosecution.
3. Civil action by Your Mortgage Company USA.
4. Civil action by other parties to the transaction, such as seller, buyer, real estate agent, Broker, or a Correspondent.
5. Employment termination.
6. Loss of professional license, if any.
7. Adverse effect on credit history.

I have read, understand and will abide by Your Mortgage Company USA Position on Loan Fraud and Misrepresentation.

Loan Officer/Loan Coordinator/Processor

By:_____

Date:_____

Printed Name:_____

Title:_____

Fraud Prevention Guide:
Fraud detection and prevention tools

AAA Insured AVM Co. insures against valuation fraud with their Automatic Valuation Model (AVM), an automated appraisal generated "within minutes" using multiple databases that cross-reference resources, leading to a "high probability" range of the value of the property. AVMs prevent both deliberate and unintentional appraisal fraud often associated with human valuations, using objectives appraisals. Reduces risk and losses that occur as a result of fraudulent representation of property value. *www.aaatrisuredaym.com* or call David Keller at 443/386.2336.

Agosoft provides loan reports to borrowers with the purpose of assuring your customers that you aren't trying to push them into the wrong loan (or a fraudulent scenario). Originators can print out the report, which details historical indexes, cost analysis, and other factors, to show borrowers that they are working diligently to meet customers' needs. The borrower can double-check the report and download the tools themselves (for up to 14 days) online *www.agosoft.com*

Appintelligence offers Web-based fraud detection, borrower verification, and quality control tools that allow originators to get a better sense of the validity of their customers' loans and applications. Products are designed to "detect and resolve data integrity, early payment defaults, fraud, and predatory issues." Appintelligence also provides fraud training sessions, either on-site or at scheduled events (such as tradeshows and conventions), as well as product training. *www.appintelligence.com* or call 363/300.2500.

Appraisal Management Company (AMCO) created Gold Seal Standard (as an add-on to its valuation and appraisal products) to comply with Sarbanes/Oxley. It incorporates a checklist of items that must be certified by AMCO personnel and the appraiser, and includes a certification statement for every completed valuation. Their Quality Review Plus product combines "proprietary methodology and algorithms" to predict the accuracy of an appraisal. *www.2.amco.net* or Neil Schneider at 800/399-2626 ext. 6058

BankersOnline.com is an online forum that brings mortgage industry professionals together to discuss and advise others on compliance, fraud, and lending regulations. Recent "threads" have included the security of borrowers sending faxes with their SSN, what to do when a customer has been red flagged, and Web site security measures. *www.bankersonline.com*

C&S Marketing is a provider of collateral risk assessment and fraud prevention software. Their chief tool, HistoryPro™, evaluates several factors to determine an "F-score" that may help originators prevent a fraudulent loan pre-funding by estimating the potential for foreclosure. HistoryPro also includes information such as property history, neighboring sales, and a transaction summary. *www.csmarketing.com*

Callender Mortgage Services conducts pre- and post-closing loan file reviews to ensure quality control. Training services for originators, processors, and underwriters address fraud detection, quality control procedures, and methods to "improve the quality of loan files." An annual on-site HUD compliance audit helps individuals and companies monitor their fulfillment of HUD requirements. Web site provides several useful industry compliance links. *www.callenderqc.com*

ChoicePoint for almost a century has been a trusted source and leading provider of decision-making information that helps reduce fraud and mitigate risk. ChoicePoint has grown from the nation's premier source of data to the insurance industry into the premier provider of decision-making intelligence to businesses and government. Through the identification, retrieval, storage, analysis and delivery of data, ChoicePoint serves the informational needs of businesses of all sizes, as well as federal, state and local government agencies. ChoicePoint keeps abreast of the issues and trends in anticipation of what we believe to be a future opportunity of risk assessment information delivery. Please feel free to contact a ChoicePoint representative at: 1-800-342-5339.

ComplianceEase Identifier™ (ID) provides identify-fraud risk management and automates Patriot Act compliance. ID also fulfills Customer Identification Program (CIP) requirements for financial accounts and allows originators to automatically detect fraudulent activity, verify identities, and provide real-time reports. Consulting and training are available as well. *www.ComplianceEase.com* or call 866-212. EASE (3273)

Fair Isaac created nine fraud prevention and detection programs, including Falcon™ ID to detect identity fraud. The product uses a variety of data sources to analyze activity and creates identity fraud probability scores for each customer.

Live (not computerized) analysts further investigate any suspicious activity. *www.fairisaac.com*

First Line Data produces Mortgage Industry Decision-Support Technology (MIDST), an instrument for risk-management and fraud prevention to perform "due diligence" that many companies and individuals overlook. Originators may find the initial approval and information tools useful in establishing quality loans. Red flag alerts call attention to particular issues within a borrower's history. *www.firstlinedata.com*

Fiserv Lending Solutions through Chase Credit offers the WebStar system, a browser-based credit reporting platform that creates merged credit reports for comparison. It also has the ability to produce AVMs to reduce human error in appraisals, flood determinations, and other specific fraud detection products. WebStar includes additional management tools as well. *www.fiserv.com*

IMARC (Investors Mortgage Asset Recovery Company) supplies fraud-related loss recovery. "Assignment" services recover losses on a contingency basis, while "Gameplan" services target-flipping schemes. IMARC seeks to not only recover losses, but also find the fraud perpetrators and prevent future fraud. *www.mortgagefraud.com*

Ingrian Networks encrypts borrowers' data to ensure security and reduce the risk of fraud, particularly through identity theft. Information such as Social Security numbers, credit information, addresses, and even e-mail can be coded to prevent unauthorized people from gaining access to sensitive data. May protect against outside hackers as well as internal fraudsters. Encryption can apply to Web sites, databases, and more. *www.ingrain.com* or call 650/261.2400

Mortgage Asset Research Institute (MARI) created the Mortgage Fraud Alert System (MFAS) for subscribers, as a fraud "early alert" service. MFAS subscribers submit alerts regarding emerging patterns of alleged fraud in its early stages of development, allowing others to detect and prevent similar attempted fraud. *www.mari-inc.com*

Mortgage Bankers Association has set up a new fraud prevention and education Web site, complete with fraud alerts to help originators stay abreast of recent fraudulent activity, a products and services directory, and information on what MBA is doing to prevent fraud. *www.mortgagebankers.org/MBAFightsFraud*

Mortgage Fraud Blog: Rachel M. Dollar, a mortgage-focused lawyer based in California, created *www.mortgagefraudblog.com* to bring attention to mortgage fraud nationwide. Recent cases are featured on the home page; state-by-state listings and fraudulent activity by category include a more comprehensive account of past mortgage fraud. The site also offers e-mail updates and search capabilities.

Platinum Data Solutions has a line-up of fraud prevention products, including Collateral Expert, which reviews property information from a variety of sources. The program can help detect property flipping, as well as undisclosed relationships between buyers and sellers. Collateral Expert works both as a stand-alone product and as an integrated component of an LOS. *www.platinumdatasolutions.com*

Risk Mitigation is a national compliance management firm which provides professional, advisory, and consulting services to financial institutions, mortgage bankers, and consumer lending entities. Our expertise addresses all critical areas associated with regulatory matters, compliance, and quality control. RMG can assist clients in meeting the oversight of regulators, fair lending mandates, and maintaining internal lending integrity and validation practices through independent quality control audits. www.riskmitigation.net or call Dr. Gary Lacefield at (817)783.7788

Rapid Reporting provides pre-funding income and identity verification products designed to help mortgage related companies combat fraud. The core offerings are IncomeChek, which is used to verify income using information provided by the IRS and DirectChek, which is used to verify identity using a combination of public database information and definitive information from the Social Security Administration. *www.rapidreporting.com*

Real U Guide to Identity Theft is a 64-page book from Frank Abagnale, author of Catch Me If You Can, which illustrates the keys to avoiding identity theft. The book is written for consumers, explaining common scams with a focus on protecting yourself, reading a credit report, and fraud awareness. *www.realuguides.com*

The SRS Group performs pre-funding audit services for lenders on an outsourced basis, in order to mitigate loss before the loan is funded. Quality assurance services done with a "human touch" are designed to catch the signs of fraud and misrepresentation that automated systems may not find. SRS also offers post-close quality control services to detect and avoid fraud through investigation and auditing on closed loans. *www.srsgroup.com* or call 800-773-1743

Sysdome encourages accountability among brokers with a broker scoring system to "demand the creation of better standards among originators." Scoring relies on current licensing status, derogatory state licensing information, a National Fraud Protection Database (NFPD) search, OFAC compliance with the U.S. Patriot Act, Sec. 23, extensive fraud and predatory lending research, lender/industry sanctions search, SafeCheck™ SSN verification for principals, bankruptcy search, and industry and client watch lists. *www.sysdome.com* or call 800-313-6751.

Teletrack, Inc. specializes in subprime consumer credit information. Monitoring services include Account ALERT Service, which creates notifications of changes in a borrower's status in real time. Their SkipGuard product warns if an applicant has obtained multiple loans within a recent time frame as well. Standard verification, scoring, and background searches are also available. *www.teletrack.com*

TruApp allows originators to scan loan files for potential fraud by searching its own historical database of fraud involving the originator, appraiser, borrower, and property. Also screens for property flips, inflated sales prices, inflated valuations, borrower identity fraud, non "arms-length" transactions, and unlicensed appraisers and/or those under disciplinary constraints. *www.truapp.com*

VMP offers a range of compliance services, including forms automation technology, regulatory compliance support and services, Internet delivery and fraud management, documents, and other lending materials. Their IDFlag™ product is designed to combat identity fraud in particular. *www.vmpmtg.com*

Verification Bureau is a leader in providing <u>fraud prevention</u> and <u>data verification</u> services for financial institutions nationwide. Our suite of web based tools is powered by the most reliable data sources and supported by the latest technology in a safe and secure data environment. Contact *Juan Carlos Perdomo-VP Sales@ 877-477-4506 x201 jcperdomo@taxverificationbureau.com* or www.verification-bureau.com

Source of information is partly from the July2005 issue of
www.mortgageoriginator.com

About the Author:
Michael S. Richardson, founder and CEO of Primero Home Loan

Michael S. Richardson speaks from experience. As president of his own mortgage and real estate companies, he discovered that one of his long-time, trusted employees was committing fraud right under his nose. Michael has been an entrepreneur since 1980 and successfully started and sold 7 businesses. He has been a loan officer, real estate agent and mortgage company owner. He has been a member of NAMB and MBA; has previously served on the Advisory Board of Fannie Mae Colorado Partnership Office; Colorado Housing Council; Colorado Mortgage Lenders Association; Commissioner of a Housing Authority board, the Board of Realtors® and won the HUD Best Practices Award. You can learn more about Michael and the various services and products he offers at his website: www.preventmortgagefraud.com.

For Current Contact information:

www.preventmortgagefraud.com
michaelr@preventmortgagefraud.com

978-0-595-37237-9
0-595-37237-6